ARRIVAL PRESS

THE BEST OF ARRIVAL PRESS
VOLUME 1

Edited by

TIM SHARP

First published in Great Britain in 1997 by
ARRIVAL PRESS
1-2 Wainman Road, Woodston,
Peterborough, PE2 7BU
Telephone (01733) 230762

HB ISBN 1 85786 680 0
SB ISBN 1 85786 675 4

FOREWORD

The poems contained in this anthology have been selected on merit by a panel of judges, the poems have been taken from a selection of books published by Arrival Press over the last 18 months.

Each judge has selected on various criteria such as content, rhythm, style and entertainment value.

I hope that whilst reading this collection you will come to appreciate the variety contained within *The Best of Arrival Press Volume I.*

Tim Sharp
Editor

CONTENTS

Our Beautiful World

People who kill for gain, have no shame
Whenever there is a profit to be made
Indirectly, we are all to blame
For not protesting against the sale

We sit in our home and watch TV
Tut in disgust, when they fell another tree
We don't want windows made of UPVC
So where does the wood come from, you tell me.

Many wild animals are on the decline
It is up to us, to make sure they survive.
Once they are dead and no longer exist
You can be sure, we'll be next on the list.

A lot of our cities resemble the jungle
The strongest rise and the weakest tumble
Leaving the scavengers to pick at their bones
Where they rot and decay in the undergrowth

To escape the smell of the rotting flesh
Those who can afford to, move where the air is fresh
What will they do, when there is no more room
Buy themselves a ticket, to fly to the moon

Leaving behind them the rest of mankind
To live in the world that they have designed
If man can do this, to his fellow man
What chance have animals, in another land

Unless we radically change our ways
Of living our lives each and every single day
We are going to end up like the dinosaurs
No, not extinct, but on all fours.

Linda Tosney

My £10 Wager

I'm not the greatest cook, there's been.
But on my day, I am quite keen.
One day I tried to make a cake,
A £10 wager was at stake.
So donned, with apron, eggs, and flour,
I hit the kitchen, on the hour.
I mixed, I baked, the hours passed.
My cake was ready, at long last.
Upon the plate, it looked a treat,
The time had come, for us to eat.
My friend, and I, picked up, and chewed,
We ate a little, but then we spewed.
You see, I'd made one tiny fault,
Instead of sugar, I'd used salt.
But to my friend, that fault was major,
And on those grounds, he won our wager.

Christopher A J Evans

The Food Fight

Marmite, Marmite everywhere,
On her blouse and in her hair,
But Alison is so well liked
Mark had better run for his life.

Some curry flew into Mark's face,
Leo said it was a disgrace,
He cooked the curry for an hour
Trying hard not to make it sour.

A funny thing to try to do,
To put yoghurt into Mark's shoe.
And while he was dealing with that
A raw egg on his head went splat.

The sign that says, 'No food fights'
Is covered now in egg and rice.
This is Mark's very worst bad dream,
Someone's got a tub of ice-cream.

Malcolm Lisle

The Night Sky

Still darkness of the night
When sky dawns her black evening gown
Aglow like diamonds the stars sparkle
I think of folks in city streets
Who see little of the sky
Their view is the fairy lights that shine
From towering blocks on high
When I look through my window
Oh lucky, lucky me, I see the cattle
Sheltering 'neath the weeping willow tree.

There in God's vast mantle above
God controls universal domain
Moon by night man shall not smile
Nor yet the sun by day.

Man's made a mess of earth and sea
Cruelty pollution continually
Man on the moon, yes we did see.
To inhabit the moon, God says
'No! That cannot, cannot be.'

Frances Gibson

Pooh

When children play
On holiday
A safe, clean site is the key,
We usually reach
A smelly beach
Where sewage pours into the sea.

Beaches are dumps
For squishy, brown lumps
Where waters froth and foam,
This with bad taste
Of other yuk waste
Makes us want to rush home.

We wonder why
The animals die
People ignore the connection,
Just from one swim
The outcome is grim -
Illness, disease and infection.

So, what do you do
When faced with pooh
Floating by your side?
Stay composed
Keep your mouth closed
And *never* open it wide.

Celia Hooker

OFFICE PARTY

The office party's in full swing.
Sausage rolls upon the floor.
Mince pies on the ceiling.
Some ladies that got drunk
Are now all too revealing.
There's someone in a locker.
Swilling all the beer.
Secretary's looking bewildered
He said to meet him here.
Our Boss's asleep on the copy machine
The lads have turned it on
'And who's that wearing a toilet seat?'
'Don't know where he's from!'

Diane Norman

DISASTER

Gale force winds wreaked havoc that day.
Beached a tanker in the bay.
The crew had fled and left it bare.
Rescue folk could only stare.
Its fate was sealed and worse yet
For oil it carried and did emit
Over bird and seal and beach.
A might lesson to us teach:
Safer mcthods must be found,
No more ships to run around.
The cost to nature is too great,
So let's change now before it's too late.

George Bailey

THE OZONE

We are burning holes
in the big blue sky.
The ozone layer
is soon to die.
Chemicals and fumes
fill the air.
Do we the humans
really care.
The sun shines through
not filtered out.
Burns our skin
do we still doubt.
Ultra rays will burn the earth
what of our offspring
what of new birth.
Freakish weather
tidal waves
flooded homes
fresh dug graves.
Dig up the scenery
build new roads
fill it with vehicles
twenty fold.
Worry now,
why who said?
when that time comes
we'll all be dead.

Jacquie Williams

STRUT YOUR STUFF

Strut your stuff in a rock 'n' roll band
While all the teenies scream;
Shout your mouth in a microphone
Shout a song hard and mean;

Strum your guitar in a rhythmic beat
Scream, jump and sing and rage;
Raise your arm, and they'll go wild
Up on the golden stage;

The joint is packed and the kids are high,
The drumbeat a pulsing clout;
Your faces sweat in the flickering light
Don't think what it's all about.

As long as the kids stream in through the door;
The kudos go in the bank;
And you can have cars and booze and fame
You've only yourself to thank.

No-one did you any favours son,
Though you did have a lucky break;
And they all want what you're giving them;
And you have a living to make.

So strut your stuff in a rock 'n' roll band,
Ride the wave while it's there,
Don't think of the future, the moment's enough
And anyway, why should you care?

Sybil Sibthorpe

Pancakes

Have you ever tried
To toss a pancake,
Take the plunge
And launch it in the air?

It looks so easy done by experts
Who toss without a care,
Manipulate the frying pan
Catching in mid air.

We had a go and
Laughed until we cried,
Our pancake failed to make it
Didn't reach inside.

Seizing on this piece of luck
A furry frame appeared
And scooped our pancake off the floor
Then vanished through the kitchen door.

No need to ask if he enjoyed it,
His wagging tail told all,
We'll have another go at tossing
And trust it doesn't hit the wall.

Jean Humphris

No Part

I have no part at all in this crazy world of ours,
No axe to grind, no pretty wife to while away the hours,
No politicians preach to me - no friends will drink my tea,
For as you walk upon the grass I'm six feet under thee.

Paul Sanders

IN THE NAME OF PROGRESS

Vast rolling hills that range across the land
Are topped by rugged rocks and tall green trees,
Huge plains and meadows reach to sloping sands
Where foamy waves form in the gentle breeze.
The sea surges a raging blue that wields
With wrath waves that crash upon the shore,
A diverse range of life this water shields,
In balance, according to nature's lore.
Above, huge clouds are blown by winds on high,
Great white airships that are always unmanned.
As gracefully they sail across the sky
Their enormous shadows pattern the land,
This great beauty within our atmosphere
Once covered each corner of the earth's sphere.

Cruel concrete now smothers the buried ground
And covers fields in mankind's own chaos,
Fumes choke all life and manic machines sound,
Proclaiming loud that nature's rule is lost.
Superfluous pollution always spills
Into even the deepest of our seas.
This is one of the eco-system's ills,
Man's wretched waste brings Neptune to his knees.
Now sulphuric fumes stain the pale blue sky
And burn away at our ozone layer.
Chemicals will cause lands to become dry,
Mankind's on course to be his own slayer.
It's too late to turn back this ticking clock
But its rotating hands we have to stop.

Chris Scriven

Party Animal

Parties? Not many!
A laugh with a few of the boys
Runnin' riot in somebody's house
And making lots of noise!

Parties? Not many!
Smoochin' into the night.
Stickin' me tongue down some tart's ear
While I'm pullin' her in, really tight.

Parties? Not many!
Gettin' well smashed on their booze
Pullin' moonies out the window
And pukin' on me shoes.

Parties? Not many!
I always try for me oats
Pull some bird then get her upstairs
Y'know, the bed with the coats.

Parties? Not many!
Gettin' some drinkin' in
Bringing a bottle of Asti Spumanti
And spending the night drinking gin.

Parties? Not many!
Gettin' totally pissed
I mean, leave it out, someone else has paid
It's too bloody good to resist!

Parties?
No,
Not many.

Steve Sutton

Innocence Lost

Never again will I feel that way,
having given myself so openly,
completely, and unselfishly.
Wanting nothing, only needing her heart,
I longed for her voice while we were apart;
but my dream never lived, it faded away
(the feelings I had, forever will stay
locked up inside me and hidden from all):
this I will hide behind a great wall,
open to none; and ne'er play the game
of love by quite the same rules again.
Don't wait by the phone - no hours in the cold
and rain just waiting for someone to hold.
Don't drown in emotion, forget empathy,
or you'll find yourself hurting and get no sympathy;
for romance is dead, it brings you no prize
when her conscience is fettered by marital ties.
Do not live in that world, you'll only get caught
in the web; and the pain that the poison has brought
will course through your veins until the end;
and nothing will soothe it, the wound will not mend,
the love that you're needing will never be there.
I won't play by the rules: I will not share
their longing and pain. Now I will take
what I want; for the rest, I will make
no room in my heart. Damned to the last,
my future has changed - my innocence, lost.

P White

Stop

This planet of ours, was a beautiful place,
It's being destroyed by the human race,
Year by year, a little more,
Humans are changing things galore,
The ozone layer has been caused by gas,
Because it was released in mass,
The temperature seems to be rising,
So the hole in the ozone isn't surprising,
Cutting down the rain forest amidst,
The forest would eat a lot of the acids
That were lurking in the atmosphere,
Now drying up, it's everyone's fear,
The power stations do it in haste,
The burning of oil, it is in waste,
Oil refineries burn off the oil,
Smoke up in the skies, takes it toll,
The dumping of waste, into the sea,
Another way to destroy, there has to be,
Toxic waste, in the water flows,
Killing all the seal life, all that shows,
The seals and whales, are getting few,
Man is killing them, for money too,
They call it progress, I call it cruel,
Can't there be a government rule?
And the car is no help to us,
It leaves a smog, the human it does,
A lot of damage, done by man,
Trying to put it right, if they can,
Get rid of the waste, find another way,
Get rid of pollution, a safe world to stay.

Lynn Hallifax

The Concrete Jungle

Here in the concrete jungle, we have all we need
Free from the restrictions of nature, we alone succeed
Down in the concrete jungle, we make all the rules
Free of our responsibilities to nature, we can act like fools
Here in the concrete jungle, we alone are king
Believing in our power over nature - we can do anything
Down in the concrete jungle, power is our goal
Ignoring the balance of nature - we gladly sell our soul

Here in the concrete jungle, we ruthlessly expand
We destroy the beauty of nature to satisfy our demand
Down in the concrete jungle, we never think twice
Rejecting the warnings of nature, we don't need advice
Here in the concrete jungle, we take, but we don't give
Abusing the laws of nature, that's the way we live

Violence! Pollution! Deprivation! Destitution!
Cruelty! Persecution! Corruption! Absolution!
Radiation! Deforestation! Exploitation! Starvation!
Hatred! Degradation! Intolerance! Indignation!

Down in the concrete jungle, power is our goal
Ignoring the balance of nature - we gladly sell our soul
Here in the concrete jungle, we take, but we don't give
Abusing the laws of nature, that's the way we live

Terry Bamforth

Stew And Dumplings

Who cares if I can't cook
What's there to know
You only follow this book
This is it I'll make a stew
I'll even make dumplings
Just to please you.
The mother-in-law's coming around her they flock
When she tastes this stew she'll be in for a shock.

She thinks I can't cook
I'll give her a surprise
It's going to be great
The best in their lives
I bought ingredients
The suet too
I piled in the veg
It looked just like glue
Oh well it smells OK
I just hope it tastes nice I cross fingers and pray

Table's set napkins are out
Bring the stew, she did shout
Everything looks lovely
Oh what a delight
But where were the dumplings
They were nowhere in sight
I put them in they'll be at the bottom
I never forget that stew it was rotten
I didn't know, flour I ad to add
my dumpling dissolved
That's why it was so bad.

There was no wonder it looked like glue
Never again it was a horrible stew
My husband couldn't eat it and he's a hog
Everyone left it including the dog.

Margaret Newton

POLLUTION SOLUTION

It seems to be the aim of man
to spread disaster as far as he can
instead of taking care of the planet
doing everything he can to destroy it.

From chemical waste to nuclear dumping
from deforestation to oil slick pumping
into the oceans and onto the land
pollution has raised a deadly hand.

The ozone layer is thinning out
because motor car rules and runs about
ever increasing in numbers and size
making clean air a treasured prize.

Now this madness has to stop
and global warming has to drop
combustion engines will have to go
or else man will be his own worst foe.

If this remedy proves too late
- the horse has gone, we shut the gate;
then our legacy to our young
will be regret at the chance we flung

Away and watch ten thousand years
could prove the worst of all our fears
and the twentieth century could be
the last of running wild and free.

So let there be a world think-pound
where problems are shared and solutions found
where differences are put aside at last
and pollution made a thing of the past.

David Robb

Why Do I Do It

Grandad, put your teeth in,
they'll all be coming soon.
I'll move that chair, from here to there,
to make a bit more room.
Bill's sure to do his *party piece,*
The *karaoke king.*
And be sure to notice and comment,
on Auntie Betty's ring.
Dad, put a clean towel out will you,
no, better make it two.
The kids will have sticky fingers,
when they've had some chocolate chew.
Jane, you take all their coats love,
and put them on our bed.
And don't get trying on Auntie Joan's fur,
if she sees you, you'll be dead.
Jim, you put out the beer mats,
Oh these glasses need a wash.
And Grandma, take your pinny off,
try to make yourself look posh.
Dad, put the kettle on, here they come,
Ouch, watch where you point that cork.
Keep the dog quite will you,
why not take him for a walk.
I won't do this again you know,
I say it every year.
But ain't it grand to see 'em all,
it brings some festive cheer.

Patricia Langton

WITHOUT YOU NOTHING COULD BE . . .

As the beautiful clear blue sky turns cold
and the tears that collect are hard to hold.
I think of all the times we had
re-seeing the memories makes me feel sad.
And all the songs I love to play
just reading the titles are hard to say.
Even the juiciest of meat
so lovely and tender is hard to eat.
And of all the drinks I love so much
although it's bubbly it's hard to touch.
All the people reach out their hands
why isn't it yours is hard to understand.
I look at all the photos of you
I feel your presence, it's hard to believe, but true.
I look in your eyes and see so much sorrow
my heart is yours forever as it's hard to borrow.
I lay in my empty bed each evening
to think you were once here is hard to believe in.
We'd be warm and cuddly and fast to sleep
now all I do is cuddle a pillow and weep.
Thoughts and thoughts going round in my mind
why was your love and trust so hard to find?
Of all the feelings in my heart
I wish we never had to part.
And all the things I've got to say
wouldn't change you in anyway.
So just one day you should listen to me
then you'd know
That Without You Nothing Could Be . . .

Fiona Frew

TENDER MOMENTS

I'd like to tell you
What happened to me
One day while I was cooking
I suppose you could say
It served me right
Because I was not looking

I had made a lot
Of banana fritters and
Some batter had stuck to the fork
What I did not know
That I would burn my lips
And would not be able to talk

My family did their best
By trying not to laugh
Told me that tea was very nice
But all that I could eat that night
Was an ice cube and a cucumber slice

Patricia Belfield

PASSAGE OF TIME

As the weeks they slowly pass
I see my face in the looking glass
And see grey hairs among the brown
Guess it's time to bring the curtain down

On being far away from you
Locked up in prison out of view
I see no sense in this here life
This confinement, these chains, this strife

So my darling I must repent
To stay by your side is my intent
When at last I'm free to go
This world and everyone I'll show

Just what makes a peace loving man
To love and provide the best I can
I'll bring to you a wealth untold
And love you while we both grow old.

Graham Malcolm Smith

EARTH FOR SALE, NEEDS ATTENTION

A consumer world, consuming the earth
Once more factory born, as a mother gives birth,
Killing of fields, as landfill sites grow,
Child's once healthy face, but now, the food has a glow.
Government steals earth, one more no entry zone,
To do tests on the hole in the precious ozone.

Decimation of forests, to the very last leaf,
For nations fast food passion for burgers of beef,
The way of the west, is the way the rest want to live,
Many more millions, will take, but what will they give,
People living their dreams, all is peaches and cream.
A planet like Hollywood, life is a scream,
Till the dawn, of a nightmare, but will we awake,
Or will nature unbalanced, finally fall and then break.

The fate of the earth lies within our own power,
Do we rise to the challenge, or do we just sit and cower,
And wait for the new age, a second chance, a rebirth,
If we do, we'll be waiting till the end of the earth.

Jeffrey Crossley

It's a Chef's Life

What is this life if it is so fickle?
You have no time shallots to pickle.
And you spill the consommé from the ladle,
Before you get it to the table . . . from the cookpot.

You try to make a nice plum pie,
And build the centre very high.
Can't understand the criticism said,
Discover you used prunes instead . . . you're a crackpot.

And now, let's try to bake some bread,
You knead and knead till it's time for bed.
Forget the tins near the oven door,
It's risen all over the kitchen floor . . . use your loaf.

That streaky bacon's rather skinny,
Fat splashes all over your plastic pinny.
And don't expect to get a handshake,
For an omelette looking like a pancake . . . you're no egghead.

A simple desert - a pink blancmange?
Resembles more of a bathroom sponge.
Your girlfriend made it - (cor! What a looker)
She let it boil all over the cooker . . . use Vim not vigour.

December's here - make a Christmas pud'n',
Mix it properly so it's no dud'n.
Take your time, take care, don't fiddle,
How could it collapse like that in the middle? . . . Give it to Santa.

As shown on telly, as a last resort,
At intervals, have a swig of port.
Something's making you feel quite dizzy,
And that spaghetti's looking fizzy! . . . Just forget it

Take that silly hat off and go back to being a motor mechanic . . .

Freda Baxter

Cry Of The Dolphins

We dolphins let out our mournful cry,
'*Please* don't let our planet die.'
We have lived so long as you may know,
We have watched man come and watched him grow.
Your discoveries have been great and promised great joy,
Now they threaten to destroy.

Your youngest child discards cans and breaks jars,
Whilst your older kind pumps poisons from cars.
The female of your species is not alone,
She uses her sprays and kills the ozone.
We *try* to tell you and you pretend to hear,
You say we are clever but still we fear,
That this beautiful world once made so pure,
Cannot much longer seem to endure,
Its animals killed off in the name of science,
Missiles and bombs built in sheer defiance.
Its beaches covered with thick tanker oil,
The sea life destroyed and its sky you spoil.
The beautiful beasts of the jungle are slayed,
For their ivory, skin, and coats displayed.
Slowly you cover each small piece of land,
With houses and factories - don't *you* understand?
That the more you take from this once lovely earth,
The less it can give as it loses its worth.
Slowly you kill it and all it contains,
Till only dry dust and ashes remain,
Look after it humans and like us give a cry,
But do something *we cannot* and don't let earth die!

B H Dance

My Last Farewell

(In dedication to Sylvia, my wife, my life)

I've often wondered, what happens when we die
Can we watch our own funeral from on high?
I don't want to know what people will say
But I want to hear while I may

If I was to say I'm really nice
Some would remark to us that cuts no ice
Eccentric I would describe, but in a nice way
Giving help to anyone and good on every day

Not good looking, but a decent sort
But funnily enough wasn't fond of sport
Played a fair game of Petanque
But his blinking old pipe stank

Always good and ready for a natter
Time to him didn't seem to matter
Helpful to all if he could
I suppose I must have done some good

He's not gone to heaven some would say
No like an oddball he went the other way
But to myself I would say I've been great
He's gone upwards to repaint the golden gate

Always with a cheerful smile
Never a misery never used guile
He would help you out come what may
Being useful made his day

Ready always to do a good turn
He would even let you share his urn
He'd go out of his way, and feel great
And kindly step aside while you they would cremate

And if the fire did peter
He'd ask God for another coin for the meter.

Prince Rhan of Kathari

Manic Destruction

Man's progress planet earth has regressed
Violation of the land and sea repressed
The beauty and life the earth once bore
That we pitiful humans can never restore

Machines and technology have taken their toll
Life and work made easy for man
This so-called progress and knowledge
Has interfered with nature's balanced plan

Her trees and foliage have been replaced
Many of earth's creatures now displaced
Factories, towns, and man-made dams
Have sprung up as if by magic to cover the land

Air that once was clean and sweet
Polluted by the vehicles that fill our streets
The water once so sparkling and pure
Filled with effluence teems with life no more

Even the sea that vast mysterious space
Cannot escape from pollution and nuclear waste
Instead of heeding the bright flashing signs
We carry on as usual - close our eyes to our crimes.

Elizabeth Amery

Party Time

Balloons in a bunch,
a bowl of punch.
Family gathered round
with smiling faces
and joyous embraces,
listening to the sound of
the pumping, pounding music
vibrating through the room.
Throbbing in my eardrum
with a consistent pulsing boom.
Is this real music?
I ask myself ponderingly.
In future, I think I'll stay at home
for it's not my cup of tea.
They're all chatting so loudly
I can't hear myself think,
before I came here
I felt in the pink.
I'm best drinking more slowly,
for it's my turn to get the round.
So I'll slip out now quietly
and not make a sound.

Beatrice Jackson

She Tried

She tried so hard to live.
She tried so hard to love.
She tried so hard to do her best
With us and God above.

She tried to bring the sunshine
Where often there was rain.
She tried to be a panacea
When another was in pain.

She tried to be so helpful,
But often made things worse.
She tried to write her feelings down
In really awful verse.

She tried to fight all battles
And oh how much she cried
When it often seemed to no avail,
But oh how much *she tried!*

Bill Baird

Homeless

Cold is the winter that's wrapped round the days,
Gone are the flowers that flourish in warm sunny rays.
Think of the people, who have nowhere to go,
We all complain, but they have nothing you know
Shelter from the cold with paper and card,
And we're all moaning that our lives are hard.

There should be a place for everyone to live
have we lost the things that we can give?
Love is precious and it should be evenly spread
think of the homeless why are we warm in our bed?
Is it so hard to stop and think
they are cold, hungry and blue, we're nice and pink?

They have no money they live from the street
we pass them by nothing warm on their feet
We see only in them things which are bad
we throw away most things what they never had.
Give them their homes and food to eat
you never know their shoes could fit your feet
And cold is the night it cuts very deep
think of these people, then you can weep.

Margaret Newton

SHE WATCHES

The day is breaking into little bits
And she is no older
Than the rocks on which she sits,
Rocks which are stained
As she watches
The day like revolution has waned.

A fading sheet of black sky
Descends over the ocean and rocks,
She takes a handful of red sand from the hot clime
And slowly wonders why
The earth has to pay this time.

A fisherman sails out his steaming boat
But it will not stay afloat
And all the fish
Swim out of the sea,
The ocean's spirits has been drunk
Leaving a landscape of worthless junk.

Still she watches and follows the sky
Waiting for it to die,
And as the workers and miners are turned up
The day is torn into little strips
Another piece of green is cut away
Another person exits his stay.

James Norman

JIM'S PARTY

My friend Jim makes home brewed beer
It doesn't seem that strong.
Each time he hosts a party
I always go along.

Do I really have to go?
Do I really have to drink?
He always says, 'This one's all right'
I won't say what I think!

Filled with good intentions,
I say, 'I'll try just one.'
That turns to three or maybe four,
This party seems like fun!

Once in bed, it's straight to sleep.
Wake up at half past three.
Hammer blows inside my head.
Feel rotten as can be.

Next morning trying all those cures,
With slim chance of success.
Aspirin, water, orange juice,
I don't know which one is best.

The headache's gone, I'm feeling fine.
Shan't do that again!
'There's a party here on Saturday.'
God! That Jim's a pain!

Alan Potter

Social Graces

I'd like to go to parties,
To be a social hit,
But parked by Maseratis
My 2CV won't fit.

I lack the social graces.
I'm no good at small talk.
Watching other people's faces
I feel a total dork.

They ask me what I'd like to drink.
Their amusement I'd see.
I wonder what they really think
To learn that I'm TT.

Then at the buffet table,
I choose what I'd like to eat
But find that I'm not able -
Failing the balancing feat.

My knife, it wobbles off my plate.
My fork jumps to the floor.
My glass rocks in a nervous state
And I search for the door.

I make my way through dancing crowd,
Grinning at witty jape.
I'm thankful that the music's loud
As I make my escape.

I'm not a social being,
But the private tête-à-tête
With candle light for seeing,
Is for me a better bet.

Nicky Dicken-Fuller

Our Mother Earth

Oh Mother Earth so beautiful,
You give us life so rare;
With nature in its many forms,
On land and sea and air;
But man's great greed has made you sad
By cutting down your trees;
And taking all your mineral wealth,
And pillaging your seas.
The water that was once so clear,
Is now unfit to drink;
And man's great greed and jealousy
Has brought him to the brink,
Of devastating conflict,
That threatens all of life;
And if we do not heed the signs,
That are so clear to see,
Mother Earth will fight back soon
To free herself of strife,
With earthquakes and with tidal waves,
And thunderstorms severe,
To try and save this world of Hers,
And all that She holds dear;
So man can start again some day
Much wiser than before,
To enjoy the wealth of Mother Earth
And respect Her much much more.

Francis A Watson

THE NIGHT BEFORE

Listing the answers
Hot from the phone,
From jesters to dancers
To garnish the home,
Where giggles and glances
Will thrill to the bone.

Stalking the packs
On the store party racks,
Too stretched and excited
To know what it lacks,
That comes without warning
In trolley fast tracks.

Candles and flowers
CD's stacked as stone,
Counting the hours
Where caution is thrown,
To excitement that towers
In planning alone.

To bed full of dreaming
That things will go well,
Cork-screw left gleaming
And cheesecake cream smell,
The week long scheming
Awaits the door bell.

Michael Faulkner

No More Tears

A land that belongs to no-one
A war that nobody's won
At the setting of the sun
A soldier picks up his gun
While a sniggering child pokes fun
I see the pain you feel
I see the sorrow
I hope and pray tomorrow
Holds no more horror
Over the years
There's been an ocean of tears
Will peace take away their fears?
I pray for no more tears.

Nicholas L Fletcher

Vanishing Childhood

They are not old but seem so old,
They are not old but look so old,
Their eyes are old, yet are not old,
Their speech, their mannerisms should
not be old, yet are so.
They lack the spontaneity of youth,
And yet should have it so,
For they are the young
Who seem so old.
What have we done,
The old who are old,
To make the young,
Who should be young,
Seem so old?
Where has childhood gone?

Patricia Willgrass Holmes

INHUMANITY

In the darkness of his Third World mine
Man rages as he scratches for time.
Marks the boundaries in blood so red
His bloated inhumanity fed.
He sits upon the laden table
Kicks away the chairs
Feasting on the starvings' cries
And the gaunt and hungry stares.
He laughs this parasitic leech
Then casts the runes in children's bones.
His inhumanity finely honed.
Making love to his own craven image
Turned on by the blood and carnage.
Justifying his inhuman whims
By the colour of another's skin.
He throws his vipers into the pit
Curses bitterly when he gets bit
Destroying himself with festering wrath
Creating his own behemoth.
Man leaves us all eternally damned
By his inhumanity towards his fellow man.

Alene Kimm

TOMORROW I'LL DIET

Tomorrow I'll diet
Today I had to keep the kids quiet
Cream cakes while I relax
And then a long, hot soak in a nice bath.

Tomorrow I'll diet
Today just one last fry up
Didn't want to see the bacon go to waste
Just one more rasher I had to taste.

Tomorrow I'll diet
Gateau on special offer, had to buy it
Also ice cream, two packs for the price of one
Goodness knows I'll end up with an even fatter bum!

Sarah Armstrong

Shifting Sand

The beauty of the silver sand
spread out as if by magic wand,
Each little breeze the sand will move
as on its own it seems to rove,
With stormy seas it's wet and slick
the wind and waves miss not a trick,
To play upon the Sandy beach
always there in easy reach,
Sand so fine it's almost dust
sometimes dark and stained with rust,
From anchor chains buried deep
the dark brown colour starts to seep,
The tide rolls in the colours change
It begins to show its varied range,
From course to fine its texture feels
as in the sand a body kneels,
With children sand becomes a toy
a different one to each girl and boy,
On day a castle then a crown
as the tide rolls in it all falls down,
Storms blow up the beach was bare
but now it's dressed with lots to wear,
Debris thrown up on the shifting sand
Is now spread out across the land.

B M Daubney

Faith

We all have a dream
So we plan and scheme
To make it come true
But it will not always do.
If we wear a frown
Then we stay down
And perhaps with a smile
In a little while
Good fortune will come your way
And hopefully always stay
It needs faith, 'tis true
But that's not too hard for you
Just get up and so
You have another go
And from now on
Your life could be *bon*.

E N Bell

Happy Jake

'Special Needs' that dreaded phrase, confirming all our fears.
Oh the heartache, disappointment, the angry bitter tears!
And yet, our darling Jakey, you have brought such fun, such joy,
That yes, there's no denying you're a *special* little boy.
Special in the way you laugh, the way you hug me tight,
The *special* way you greet me, with such obvious delight.
I pray one day, we'll find the key that opens up the door
To speech, and understanding - though we couldn't love you more
If you were what the world calls *perfect* - for you are no mistake -
You will always be our darling, happy, *special* little Jake.

Elizabeth Brooker

If There's A God . . .

The thin little body racked with pain.
How can God let it happen - has the world gone insane?
Famine and drought in this world of ours
Where's the miracles now and the men with power?
Arms outstretched, eyes as big as saucers.
What has she done to suffer such torture?
Helping hands reach out to embrace.
Oh God what is happening to the human race?
Tenderness, compassion, love and care
But there's not enough to go round, not enough to share.
Why is there such suffering, hunger and loss?
Ask the politicians they put it down to cost.
Why does it cost money to help people in need?
So God cut the crap . . .

Listen to the prayers . . .

take heed.

Gena McCrystal

So Long Shorty!

I've snuffed it, I thought I'd never go
I've kicked the bucket, it's the end of my show
Maybe I'll go to heaven, I just don't know
I wasn't as good as gold or as white as snow
I lived my life that's all you need to know
I was happy with my life, I thank the soul
who stole my wife
I'm not glad I've gone, also not sad.
So long!

John Beals

IT COULD HAVE BEEN EDEN . . .

There once was a time when forests grew, lush and green and rife.
Breathing unpolluted air we believed was a way of life.
Eating the meal upon our plate without the fear of harm
instead of contamination, instead of the ruined farm.
We could have had an Eden, we could have had it all
we are simply the caretakers, not the Lord of the Hall.
Nature has given us all we need, all is there if we seek.
But we think that we're the masters. We're children, and we're weak.
We label our problems 'environment,' ask where the problems start?
It was us, *we* raped the planet, and tore out her loving heart.
And when we yell pollution, carcinogens and the like,
we put them there, not nature. *We* made the deadly strike.
We slashed and burned the forests, we contaminate the soil
we gouged out her coal and peat and wood, made her spew out
the precious oil.
Look at the sun! We don't see warmth or friendliness or hope
but melanomas, cancers, oh, there's such a lot of scope.
We're playing with radiation - nothing to see or feel
nothing to hear or touch my friend. At least, not until you're ill.
Then you can see what man has done, in his apocalyptic way
he's messed into what he shouldn't, a delinquent brat at play!
We've shown just how much she can trust us, we've opened a hole in
the sky.
How much bigger does it need to be until we all start to fry?
She gave us everything we need, the forests, the pastures, the sea
the rivers and streams the mountains and dales, an Eden for you and
me.
All *we* had to do was love her, this wonderful planet called earth.
More effort, more planning, less stripping her bare, let's try
for all that we're worth.

Or all that we'll leave to the future, all that remains of this glory
will fade into desolation, where they'll tell of the trees as a story.
Along with the grass and the flowers, together with brooks and the
seas,
legend is all that we vandals will leave, instead we should drop to
our knees.
And pray there is still a flicker of hope, and that we can right the sin
of erasing the things that make living worthwhile, and try to learn
how to begin.

Rosemarie Varndell

MANKIND ON TRIAL

The trees now burnt
The bracken bare
Where once nature's beauty had been seen
Now an empty barren wasteland
Lies deserted of life
Upon our planet earth.
Its atmosphere now poisoned
By polluted skies
Unclean
Forests decaying
Rivers run dry
Contaminated oceans now destroyed
By the hand of man
Society's shame
Questions must be asked
Who is to blame?
Before the end result
Is the destruction of earth itself.

Arthur Harvey

A CHILD WONDERS

I wonder why the earth is round
When to me it looks quite flat.
I wonder why the sky is blue
There must be a reason for that.

I wonder why the grass is green
And why trees grow so tall
I suppose it would not be quite right
If the same things applied to all.

I wonder why dinosaurs became extinct
After millions of years of existence,
Why microbes seem to go on forever
There seems no end to their persistence.

I wonder when the world will end
In God's good time, or ours?
There's so much atomic energy round
And in the hands of so many Powers.

I wonder why we have to die
Why our time on earth's so short
To take our place in Heaven or Hell?
At least, that's what I've been taught.

I wonder why there's so much hate
Cruelty, pain and greed
And in a world of plenty
Man's caused so very much need.

I really wonder what God must think
Of how man's treated His planet
He intended it to be His pride and joy
Since the day when He began it.

William M Jones

Fudge Toffee

We made fudge toffee, my brother and I,
Aunty had made some and it was swell,
If she could do it, so could we
With a lasting supply of sweets as well.

When mum was out we raided the larder -
2 oz of butter, 2 tablespoons of syrup,
2 oz of sugar, a tin of condensed milk,
And boil together until 5 mins is up.

The aroma was strong and finger-licking sweet,
Then we found mum's baking tray to grease,
We poured in the bubbling stickiness
And couldn't wait to try a piece.

We left it under the bed to cool,
But when we came to break it away,
The toffee had set just like concrete
And we couldn't get it out of the tray.

So we borrowed dad's chisel and hammer
But the toffee was as hard as sin,
We managed to break it in pieces,
But we made awful holes in the tin.

The time that we made fudge toffee -
It took hours to suck and chew,
And mum went spare when she saw the tray
And the spoon and pan stuck like glue.

Esme Francis

THE HEDGEHOG

I hear a snuffle, a rustle on the ground,
A funny little shuffle, from under the mound,
From leaves and moss poke a tiny snout,
He gives a sniff and two shiny eyes look about.
Where's his courage, he's timid and shy.
Many sharp spines appear, he looks to the sky.
The moon gives a shiny path in the dark,
Gives to small beady eyes a bright spark.
Spines glisten as he moves on the grass.
Smelling milk on a dish makes him bold as brass.
Dew forms on grass and on some leaves,
Hedgehog passes under with some ease.
Drops fall on his black nose and back.
He rolls into a ball, from the watery attach.
His spines stick out, sharp and long,
Until he's convinced there's nothing wrong.
When he's sure he's safe from harm,
Another noise gives him alarm.
Something moves in light of day,
Long and slim, its in his way.
Slithering along the ground is a snake,
It is an adder, there's no mistake.
A banquet in the long green grass,
Mustn't let this reptile pass.
He attacks, then rolls up tight,
Then he'll take another bite.
Back and fore till the snake is dead.
Now to rest - the hedgehog's fed.

Josie Minton

The World

An eternity of existence,
Horizontally, vertically prevailing.
Provider of life,
Yet in different ways.

Life starts in society,
For others in a slum.
Clean sheets in a hospital,
Water from the river.

Cities, jam-packed and alive.
Comforting little villages.
Dirty streets of India,
A township in South Africa.

A life full of dreams,
For some a desperate struggle.
Some work for a living,
Others relax in the sun.

Some greedy and heartless
Too rich to care.
The poor live on basics,
Street kids on theft.

All elements of one world.

Katie Sumner

Poverty Knocks

poverty knocks
knocks for the elderly
knocks for the sick
knocks for the unemployed
knocks for society's misfits
poverty knocks

poverty knocks
knocks for large families
knocks for ethnic minorities
knocks for the handicapped
knocks for the low-waged
poverty knocks

poverty knocks
knocks for the under-eight's
knocks for claimants
knocks for widows
knocks for the redundant
poverty knocks

poverty knocks
knocks for single parents
knocks for the homeless
knocks for women
knocks for jobless youth
poverty knocks

poverty knocks
from a few
always with us
millions are knocking with bloody knuckles
can't you hear the din?
poverty knocks

P Kemp

I Don't Feel Well

I'm under the weather
And down in the dumps
I've not got the flue
And I'm sure it's not mumps
But I just don't feel well!

I've taken my pulse
My temperature too
They both appear normal
So what can I do?
I just don't feel well!

The weather's been awful
So could it be that?
I went to the doctors
And had a long chat
I told him - I just don't feel well!

He looked at my tongue
And examined my ears
Prescribed me a tonic
Allayed all my fears
But I still don't feel well!

There must be a reason
Why I feel so blue
Could this chronic feeling
Be *me* missing *you*?
I just don't feel well!

Come back to me darling
I love you so much
I know I'll feel better
With your loving touch
Without you - I just don't feel well!

Geoff Jeffries

ABANDONED DREAMS

Young man,
with your deep brown eyes
and unruly curls,
could you want me?

Young man,
with your laughing mouth
and inviting smile,
could you want me?

Young man,
with your firm young flesh
and enchanting face,
could you want me?

Young man,
with your lively mind
and vitality,
could you want me?

Young man,
with my fading looks
and abandoned dreams,
could you want me?

Sylvia Anderson

INTO ALTERNATIVES

Shiatsu and yoga, ying and yang
I'm into alternatives with a bang!
A bit of confusion for the brain
Are they all different or - the same?

Acupressure or puncture for release
Of trapped energies if you please!
Chinese herbs, so good for tension
And cider vinegar on the day of ascension.

For arthritis it's the perfect cure
No more pains for you to endure.
You may wonder about Thai Chi
It's almost made a new woman of me!

I'm also very much on the pill
Homeopathic, if you will -
So, I should be extremely well
Yet instead I ache like *hell!*

Lily Seibold

WE ALL MAKE MISTAKES

Once our planet was a beautiful place,
People did not live in the rat race.
The water ran as clear as crystal,
and life was lived at a leisurely pace.
Vegetation was lush and green,
the rivers, oceans and seas were clean.
Lots of fish and crustaceans,
Dolphins, whales and seals, (not mutations)
They cut down the rain forests,
but did not plant more trees.
So mud slides wiped out whole communities.
They found a hole in the ozone layer,
they say it's getting bigger.
So they tell us it's the gas we use in our sprays.
Scientists were given a free hand,
Their efforts have altered the natural balance of the land,
and now future generations will have to pay,
for all the mistakes made by man's way.

Kathrine Summers

Velvet

Upon soundless velvet wings
I patrol the night
Silently gliding amongst the sylvan trees
of my verdant woodland home
I am the orchestrator
of the music of the night
Beneath the velvet void of space
along ancient woodland ways
silent flight and feather softness
eyes of midnight darkness
the windows of the soul
Velvet voles and minuscule mice
watch the stars in a midnight sky
The Queen of the night drifts silently overhead
Moonlight, moonbeams, silvery reflections
Cool darkness upon my face
beneath the full moon of winter solstice
a lunar lantern, a silver globe
long after the blue harvest moon
a velvet intermission in time.

Brenda Straw

The Postman

A young man's coming down the street,
The mail upon his back:
Through rain or hail, or snow or sleet
He struggles with his sack.

A postcard from the South of France
Sent by a widow's son,
A letter full of bright romance
And bills for everyone.

No matter what the contents be
Or where they have to go,
He'll struggle through adversity
'gainst any winds that blow.

To him his duty is quite clear
To serve both me and you,
To march along without a fear
And make the Mails go through.

Mervyn Whale

EPITAPH FOR A RAILWAY ENTHUSIAST

Here lies the frame
of old what's-his-name,
who built up a dream
founded on steam.
Steam in his soul, steam in his blood,
steam in his heart. It did him no good.

For when steam arose
in front of his nose
it clouded his eye . . .
the world passed him by.
Steam for his breakfast, steam for his tea,
steam for his dinner. It filled him with glee.

Ne'er did he stray
from this permanent way.
Gricing through life
he scarce knew his wife.
A narrow gauge mind, or so it would seem,
and now passed away like a man made of steam.

Horace Gamble

THE HOLOCAUST

This happened many years ago
Before we were all born,
We don't seem to realise
What they all saw.

It all started in 1933
With Jews' privileges taken away
No more Jewish shops
The Jews were no longer free.

In 1941 the final solution was made,
To concentration camps
They were taken and split up
And God help them if they disobeyed.

The weak were taken to gas chamber
And told to undress,
To leave behind all possessions,
In 12 minutes they would be dead,

The strong were taken away
To work in the cold,
With no food and no warmth,
No longer allowed their own say.

In 1942 more laws were enforced
That the Jewish schools
Would be closed
And no more groceries could be brought

But in 1945
An end was brought to all,
Now every nation can live as one
And never lets us brawl.

Lisa Dawson (16)

Moonbeams

Silently stealing into the room,
pillars of ivory from a cold distant moon,
cream coloured fingers searching to find,
mischief or madness in the depths of the mind.
Lying quite still on the brass coloured bed,
the shadowy images flit in the head,
evocatively sliding around on the floor,
the ceiling, walls, the back of the door.
Eyes closed tight yearning for dawning,
hands entwined praying for morning.
Can the sun offer the lunatic release,
or does the moon haunt, still defying him peace?
Slowly the warm amber glow of sunrise,
hurries the hideous out of the eyes
To lurk in the shadows, to hid in the wall,
impatiently waiting for sunset to fall.

Sharon McDonnell

Count Your Way To Slimdom

One, two, buckle my shoe . . .
Oops, I can't reach - would you?
Three, four, knock at the door
'Is this the sliming club?'
            'Yes, sure!'
Five, six, pick up sticks
Of carrot and celery for your morning fix.
Seven, eight, don't be late
For clocking in your weekly weight.
Nine, ten, and you'll be shoutin'
And your new, slim figure you'll be flauntin'.

Kate Munden

UNTITLED

Suzanne sits at the checkout
In a big supermarket
I'm outside in my mini
Trying to park it
If she's bored
Is she thinking about me?
Why does she have to leave
For University?
Let's get married
Think about it, have a fag
'Here's your receipt
Did you want that in a bag?'
We'll have a load of children
A daughter called Pearl
Stay with me forever, 'cos
I love you checkout girl.

Graeme Hewitt

FIELD MOUSE

When darkness falls,
And children sleep,
Out from its hole the mouse will creep.
Scampering across the grassy ground,
It hopes that it will not be found.
But up up high upon a branch,
A nasty owl saw his chance.
He swooped down low
And caught the mouse,
And took him to his comfy house.

Lauren Stanley (9)

THE MORNING AFTER

11.00 Saturday
who is this next to me in bed?
I'd turn to look but Oh my head
is full of heavy heavy rocks
which shake at the sound of ticking clocks
(don't even mention the alarm)
I've obviously done myself some harm
That punch was lethal that's for sure
So why did I go back for more?
Well it tasted nice
and fruity too
But look at what it's made me do
(so just who is he?) don't ask me
I haven't got the faintest clue
I'm not sure just what did I do
I can't remember that's for sure
behaviour like this I really abhor
It's just so sordid don't you agree?
(Oh he's waking up . . . asking for tea)
Jeff - it's only Jeff who I've fancied like mad
this really hasn't turned out bad
Oh lucky lucky me
Come over here and sod the tea!

Saudade Peon Mauraii

PUBLIC ENEMY PETER

Here before you
Is Peter Houghton's grave,
renowned in life
for his refusal to shave.

With old-fashioned hair-do
and scruffy old clothes,
biting his nails
and picking his nose!

His bad habits followed
wherever he went,
infuriating people
all the hours that God sent!

Clicking his fingers
whenever he got bored -
and when he went to bed
he deafeningly snored!

Shunning the bath tub
and even the shower,
but according to him
he smelt like a flower!

He loved to wander
and travelled on foot,
and now that he's dead
we just hope he stays put!

P Houghton

EPITAPH FOR A JOKER

Here lies one who loved to frighten
To creep upon and thus enlighten
The husband dear, one's pride and joy
Whose mother frightened when a boy
With tales of ghosts in country lane
Of soldiers in some battle slain.

I've hidden in some weird places
Struck terror to so many faces
And even realised with glee
My daughter now takes after me
And scares her husband something rotten
Right out of his nice socks of cotton.

If you should see me now I've gone
I'd like you just to dwell upon
The fact I never meant you harm
For really I was full of charm
A lovely soul, you must admit,
Who didn't mean to cause that fit.

Yet, Oh dear love, there is a rumour
That naught destroys a sense of humour
I hope I can suppress this fooling
And not sink to those depths of ghouling
But all sedate, unseen pass on
To where the pure in heart have gone.

Enid Kronbergs

When I Am Gone

Don't mourn for me when I am gone, and please don't shed a tear,
I may be gone in body, but in spirit I will be near.
And when you walk in the garden we've loved, and flowers scent the air,
Do not be sad because I'm gone, for I will still be there.
For I had everything my love, that a man could want in life,
A lovely home, two children fair, and a beautiful, loving wife.

For life has been so good to me, throughout this golden age,
Like a wonderful true story book, with joy on every page.
And you, my ever loving wife, through your devoted care,
Helped to give me this good life, when your life you did share.
Throughout the years you've worked so hard to make our house a home,
And strived to make our love grow strong so neither one should roam.

You gave me children to delight, a son and daughter fair,
The girl with the golden ponytail, the boy blond curly hair.
And of my children I am proud that they've turned out so fine.
They both would stand out in a crowd, a joy to know they're mine.
It gave me such happiness, over the years, to watch them grow,
That I would wish that every family, on earth, could find it so.

For you my daughter, our first-born, a quiet and thoughtful girl,
So keen to help at any time, amongst others you are a pearl.
My son, so tall and handsome, with his beautiful young wife,
I'm very pleased at the way they've brought great joy into my life.
But none of this was possible, without you, my darling wife,
For you made all my dreams come true, and gave our children life.

So when you feel the summer breeze, gently caress your cheek,
I will be that gentle breeze, although I will not speak,
And if the sun should warmly shine and kiss you tenderly,
It will be no-one my dear, but your loving husband, me.
So please don't mourn when I am gone, and don't shed any tears,
Just think of all the joy we had, together, through the years.

Philip M Brown

HERE LIES WENDY

Here lies the body of an unknown writer,
she never gave up, her pen was a fighter.
Many poems she wrote, leaving her novel neglected,
she vowed that one day it would be written and accepted.
Accepted . . . a best seller . . . her childhood dream,
the fame and the fortune, all hers to redeem.

There never was much time to sit down and write
and then the poor soul started losing life's fight.
Sickness took over and she retired to her bed,
the words of her book going around in her head.
The book in her head died with her that day,
her unwritten words with so much to say.

And as she was nearing her impending death,
she picked up her pen as she drew her last breath.
There on the paper she shakily wrote,
her very last words . . . her very last quote.
She felt her soul leave, to heaven . . . ascend,
and scrawled on the paper her words said . . .
The end!

Wendy Nethercot

A PUN MY SOUL

Here's to the memory of Aubrey Woolman,
No genius he, but nobody's fool, man:
He enjoyed good living, liked his fun,
And never could resist a pun:
When Peter met him at the gate
And asked him if he'd kindly state
In what conviction he had died,
'I'm a *dyed in the wool man*' he replied.

Aubrey Woolman

THE DIET

Monday morning, Oh what a pain.
Stepped on the scales,
Jumped off again!
That doesn't add up,
That couldn't be right!
I was two pounds lighter, just the other night.
But that was the weekend
A time to relax you see.
When I like to sit and watch TV.
With a pack of crisps, and a chocolate bar.
But it didn't seem much,
That's just not fair!
Once again I give a sigh,
I'll give the diet another try.
I'll do it this time, just wait and see!
I'll look in the mirror,
To a new slim me!

Margaret Spiers

OSCAR'S WALLPAPER

Sometimes good
Sometimes bad
Sometimes happy
Sometimes sad
Never an ogre
Never a miser
But on the whole
Still none the wiser!

David Harrison

PEACE

Now in this grave I lie at peace,
at least that's what I hope.
No longer will I have to watch,
another thriller, quiz or soap.
No more pop music blasting out,
and causing such a din.
No noisy children, barking dogs,
or cats going in the bin.
No more working in a factory,
full of noise most of the day.
No more working fingers to the bone,
to earn such a little pay.
For here I will have peace at last,
or so the nice old vicar said.
But if I have a noisy neighbour,
then I'll get up and move my bed.

J Stephens

SILVER WEDDING

Twenty-five years, sounds a very long time
Gone in a flash like the drop of a dime.

Twenty-five years, not all heaven 'neath a spell,
But of ordinary things of which we will tell.

Twenty-five years of washing up pots,
And making the beds and changing our tots.

Twenty-five years of low spots and high,
And knowing the moment to let things go by.

Twenty-five years we have had my dear love,
May twenty-five more be blessed from above.

Alice Sherratt

Hic Iacet . . .

Here lies the body
Of old Frank Henry.
No longer here,
Now just a memory.
He was poor,
So died in penury.

Some people think
That poor old Frank
(A would-be poet)
Was quite a crank.
He scribbled verses
For a prank
And left his royalties
To pay his bank.

What a joker!
He wasn't daft.
They wouldn't pay
His overdraft!

His dying words,
So it is said,
As he lay
In his bed.

'Even if you're very ill
Do your best to leave a will.
It's better, far,
To die in penury
Than intestate!'

Frank Henry

STEPS TO HEALTHINESS

It's not always easy to keep healthy these days,
Lack of time and motivation are sometimes to blame.
With new innovations and fast foods, why should we cook?
But these are my four steps, so just take a look.

My first step is to look at what's in my diet,
Low fat and high protein are what I require,
I drink plenty of water, enjoy fresh fruit and veg,
Don't smoke or drink alcohol, they go straight to my head.

My next step to keeping healthy I find,
is knowing what's going on in my mind,
for my mind controls how I feel within,
emotions and well being have an inextricable link.

So I use relaxation as the key
to inner peace and harmony,
sometimes nerves are really put to the test
yoga and deep breathing can help ease the stress.

Step three is to concentrate on *keep fit*
a bike ride, or netball, or I go for a swim,
I make it enjoyable and team up with friends
It's a sociable event and quite a challenge.

My last step is to enjoy life and try to maintain,
a positive outlook, and I do not restrain,
from spending time with those I like and love,
and spiritually, I have faith in God above.

So these are the steps that work for me,
I have a holistic approach as you will scc,
The four steps I've mentioned, aim to combine,
a healthy body, spirit and mind.

Yvonne Wright

THE HEALTH FREAK

I do not smoke, I do not drink
I don't just sit around and think.
I don't drink coffee, I don't drink tea
Cream cakes and crisps are not for me.

I watch my diet, I watch my weight
I wait and watch, and watch and wait.
I'm so relaxed I can visualise
That eight and not eighteen's my size.

I run upstairs, I breathe in deep
I exercise even in my sleep.
I stand on my head, I touch my knees
All exercises done in threes.

I first detox and then destress
I fast and all my sins confess.
I press my temples, massage my toes
And hypnotise away my woes.

I buy up health mags by the score
While remedies down my throat I pour.
I swallow vitamins A, C, D
And E and B and B and B.

I oil my skin and oil my joints
While tracing my meridian points.
Just come and see and soon you'll be
A perfect nervous wreck like me.

Patricia A Chisholm

Salt Of The Earth

She always has a smile
And some helpful advice
Her manner is very pleasant
Her nature, sunny and nice

She listens sympathetically
To anyone in need
Never turns down an opportunity
Of doing someone a good deed

If you're feeling under the weather
She will give you lots of care
Even if depression is your enemy
She will still be there!

She will talk to you and listen
Provide the shoulder for you to cry
She doesn't sit in judgement
We often wonder why?

She will always make you laugh
As her sense of humour knows no bounds
Her popularity is endless
As folk come from miles around!

Who is this unsung hero?
The salt of this troubled earth
She's my best friend and my mother
The one who gave me birth

But she herself is in pain and disabled
Though doesn't let it stand in her way
For her philosophy of life, is . . .
To give thanks for every new day!

Sharon Goldsmith

My Bad Vice

I do not smoke I do not drink
I walk and swim and paint,
The way in which I live my life
You'd think I was a saint.

But give me a gooey chocolate bar,
A burger and some fries,
I'm not the same, I'm a different girl
You'd think I'd been telling lies.

What is it that makes me act so?
Why do they taste so good?
Why can't crispbreads be delicious?
Not taste like a block of wood.

I won't buy those cakes and sausage rolls
I really cannot resist.
Before I go to the supermarket,
I'm going to make a list.

I've been on twenty diets,
This time I'm going to win.
Instead of going in me,
The junk food's going in the bin!

D Sharp

Sue Hills - A Tribute

You've had your share of problems,
But you're never too busy to help,
We all know who to turn to,
If we need comfort or advice.

Everyone admires you,
For your kind and caring attitude,
How can we ever repay you,
For all the kindness you have shown us.

I shall never forget how you helped me,
Through the worst time of my life,
And how you continue to support me,
In everything I do.

This poem is a tribute to you,
For everything you do,
From everyone at SMYT,
But especially from me.

Lynsey Bessent

Healthy Living

Health advice from many sources
Advise the public along correct courses,
Five helpings a day of veg and fruit
Show all the way the recommended route:
It's very important - so don't forget
Consume less sugar, less salt, less fat.

A half hour's activity, three times a week
Is not a lot of time to seek
The benefits that will ensue,
Include extra energy and well-being too.

So find the desire to self improve,
The results will surely highlight the truth
That the recommendations from experts wise
Is not a load of rubbish or lies;
Keep calm, keep happy and give a smile
And tell the world that life's worthwhile.

Joan Wilson

Be Happy

Be happy, be healthy,
    be veggie, be wise.
We don't need to eat meat for
    the rest of our lives.
Delicious fresh fruit and veg,
    nuts, seeds and beans,
Are nutritious enough for us
    human beings.
Limit your alcohol to one
    drink or none,
And you will save money by
    the ton.
For your own health's sake
    and your family's too,
        no more smoking for you.
No more smelly smoke breath
    or home and clothes that reek
And look at the money you'll save
    every week.
Have fun with the family
    play games together and
        exercise,
And you will all live much
    healthier and happier lives.

June Taylor

A True Friend

I have an unsung hero,
Of whom I cannot say.
If his name I were to tell
The game I'd give away.

He hates so, to be reminded
Of the good deeds he has done.
Yet of the past he loves to hear
To tell of things to come.

He'll always be a nice young man
With those loveable thoughts he'll keep
This person I must never forget
For without him I would weep.

Tracey Anne Chafer

FRIENDS

What is a friend?
A friend is someone
Who is always there,
Who sees you are down
And is there to care.
Is straight laced yet funny,
Is complex but fair
Can be obstinate, witty,
With panache and flair.
A friend is someone
Who sees without telling,
Who calms you down
When you feel just like yelling,
Who drops in by *chance*
When you can't really go on
And when you bore them to death,
They stifle a yawn!
A friend is all things
Both loving and true
And to be such a being,
Is a friend,
Are you?

Moira Brabender

Lament

I used to be slim enough to frolic
But not now I'm a chocoholic.

I really try being extra good
And eat my fruit and healthy food.

It's all the other bits that do it
Some say, 'Don't swallow, only chew it.'

If you live alone there's none to say
'You've had your quota for today.'

Then again, if you cook for a lot
There's always left-overs in the pot.

My mother told me 'Waste not want not'
So what chances have I got?

As Shakespeare said - 'I've always felt
Oh! That this too too solid flesh would melt.'

Melt it does not, it's so sad
All the tasty things are bad.

Why can't diets be pies and sweets
With lots of cream and likewise treats?

All of *Slimming's* notes I follow-
Why do I say I'll start tomorrow?

P Reed

A Gentle Giant

I can't believe that you are gone,
I will remember you, my whole life long,
A gentle giant of a man,
So loving and kind,
Another friend like you, I'll never find,
When I had worries you were always there,
My many problems you would share.

Your laugh, your lovely smile,
You made my life seem more worthwhile,
You never showed your pain,
Courage like yours I'll never see again.

They say that there is a heaven,
I just hope that this is true,
Because if there is, I know that,
God will have reserved a place for you.

For in your life, you always did your best,
Even on the times when you didn't feel at your best,
You kept your sense of humour,
Showed your love and proved that you really cared,
And your laughter and jokes with everyone you shared.

I was so upset the day that you died,
Oh Lord how everybody cried,
But now I know that you are at peace,
And realise that death to you was a release,
For you will never again feel pain,
And so I say goodbye dear friend,
Until hopefully we will meet again.

Terri Brant

An Ode To Dieting

I'm quite an expert at dieting,
I've been doing it all my life,
I've lost weight and then put it on again,
It's caused me much anguish and strife.
I've tried acupuncture, hypnosis,
Liquid diets, replacement bars, too.
I've taken diuretics and laxatives,
And spent half my life on the loo.
I've tried every fad diet going,
Lived on grapefruits, apples and rice,
Now they're alright in small doses
But pounds every day's not so nice.
But at last I've discovered the secret
Of eating that's healthy and right,
I've switched to low fat and low sugar,
And ask before taking each bite;
Am I hungry or just being greedy,
The answer is often the last,
So I try to keep myself busy
Until the feeling has passed.
And at last I've learned a great lesson,
It's come to me in the end,
If you eat to live, not live to eat,
Food's not an enemy, but a friend.

Sandra Frost

Untitled

He slept with every girl he met
Until one day he made a bet,
He tried to woo old Mrs Stallone
And now at last he sleeps alone.

Here he lies, struck by malaria.
On his deathbed, his last question:
'So what's the death rate in this area?'
Same as everywhere, one death per person.

He always thought that to die
Was the last thing he'd do.
He was right. Here may he lie
In remembrance to me and you.

Kimbo

SHORT SPELL AT THE GYM

I thought I ought to exercise, so joined a local gym,
Big mistake, it's not for me, I know as I go in.
Muscled men all working out, I've never felt so fat,
And girls with bodies taut and firm, why can't I look like that?

I'll have a go on this machine, it seems to be for rowing,
It's not so easy breathing in, to stop my stomach showing.
I'm so self-conscious, how much more am I supposed to do,
I'm sweating freely, rosy faced, and badly need the loo.

On the treadmill next to me, a girl has run for miles,
Her hair's in place, no sweat on her (I hope that she gets piles!)
Triceps, biceps, lats and pecs, where the heck are they?
They sound like something foreign, what you'd eat on holiday.
It's all completely alien, I feel like such a prat,
I'll do my working out at home, where I don't feel like that!

Karen Sanger

PASSENGER TICKETS

I wrote away to England, to get some jeans you see,
They were my size, but when they came there was too much of me.
I got 'em past my ankles, I got 'em past my knees
But they would go no further, no matter how I'd squeeze.

The time had come I realised to lose that fat at last
I'd better lose those wobbles, my scales were just aghast!
I sat and contemplated, this heap that once was me
Can that be my tummy, with ripples like the sea?

The Slimmers' Club would help me, my friend was heard to say
Don't argue - come and slim with me, we'll do just what they say.

The scales are struggling less now, there isn't so much weight
My tickets are now *passenger* instead of *go by freight!*
The Slimmers' Club has helped us, they made us realise
That changing how we cook and eat makes us our proper size!

Linda Reeve

NOW THAT THE FIGHTING HAS STOPPED

Masses of bodies just lying around
After the fighting had stopped
Masses of poppies covering the ground
When from the planes they were dropped.

Bullet cases, empty shells
Unexploded bombs.
Crying people, lonely bells.
White crosses on the tombs.

Back to the homes we once adored
Food in the stores where we once shopped
Friendship and loving at last restored
Now that the fighting has stopped!

Richard Griffiths (13)

EXPECTED

Kids, who would have them, you're not seriously thinking of that,
The heartburn and sickness not to mention getting fat.
Your teeth go bad and your hair falls out, it's one ill after another,
Are you sure you want a baby and cope with all that bother?
Remember your nice complexion, not a blemish or spot to be seen,
A couple of weeks into your pregnancy, when you look in the
mirror, you'll scream.
It's worth it in the end, nine months is nothing to bear,
But try getting back into those jeans,
Oh no! The big belly is still there.
It's not that I want to put you off but just
Think of the inconvenience and bother,
I should know, I have experience, after all
Darling, I am your mother!

Gloria Hawthorne

THE SOMEONE

For a long time there is someone I have known,
Who is kind, considerate and understanding too,
A person whose gentle, thoughtful, caring ways have shown,
That when you are down such people can make you feel new.

For this person is always there when you are feeling down,
Their gentle, thoughtful and caring ways which help
to remove the frown,
The listening ear which makes things clear,
And for that understanding that is so sincere.

So who is this person to whom I refer?
Just take a look in the mirror and you will see,
A physical reflection of you or me,
Now take a look at your inner self and repeat after me,
As you think so shall you be.

Timm Dorsett

BRITISH TELECOM

My telephone is my life-link
Although much cheaper writing in pen and ink
BT would not agree with this
But to them I will give a miss.

Pounds and pounds to BT I have spent
And that does not include the rent
I have chattered and gossiped within my four walls
And all my money goes to BT for calls.

I must really try to stop it
As I am so much out of pocket
With people like myself BT takes the loot
And if I keep making these calls
My husband will give me the boot!

My best friend has moved from our town to the sticks
How else will we gossip, what will we do for kicks?
I think somehow BT will win
As I also have to ring my kin.

Maybe family and friends can ring me instead
Then maybe my credit would not be in the red.
My resolution is to keep the phone bills down
Then my poor husband need not read them with a frown.

Thanks BT you have been a pal in the past
But maybe I am seeing sense at last!

Ann Starling

The Silent Heroes

All that I am is a slave without thanks or pay,
I start work early in the morning until late in the day.
I have to cook breakfast, dinner and tea,
As for the washing up, it is always left to me.
I have to have all the strength I can muster,
To race around with a hoover and duster.
Washing and ironing is another little treat,
If only I had time to put up my fee.
Nurse, problem solver and advisor I have to be,
I am not a prisoner, but I am certainly not free.
I must get going the beds must be made,
But first I must see that the table is laid.
Oh! I must remember his trousers need sewing,
But it will have to wait, the grass needs mowing,
'My wife does not work,' my husband has said,
Who does he think keeps him clothed and fed?
I never have a day off, no time to be ill,
To change places with a man would give me a thrill,
Second thoughts just think of the damage,
A man could not cope, they would never manage.
So come on husbands spare a minute of your life,
Appreciate and thank your silent hero of a wife.

L Turner

On The Shelf

Here lies the body of Anne-Marie,
Died whilst busy preparing the tea,
Always in a hurry, she could not wait;
Died before her sell-by date.

Anne Sharman

OUR STEVE

There's a young man in our town
Steve Povey is his name
He makes life worth living
Makes it full of fun and games

He may not be a macho man
Or ever saved somebody's life
Just an ordinary man really
With children and a wife

But he does such a lot for charity
And he's a hero to us in Leek town
Mediaeval days and Moorlands Theatre
And he loves acting the clown

Moorlands Theatre is for our youngsters
It keeps our teenagers off the streets
They put together plays, with themselves acting
And they always raise the seats

Steve doesn't like to take much credit
For all his fund raising and all his work
But we know without Steve Povey
Leek town would be in the lurch

I also went to school with Steve
Back in those good old days
And it never occurred to me then
One day I'd be singing his praise

So Steve's our unsung hero
He is the one I nominate
Because to everyone here in Leek town
Steve Povey is a real mate.

Heather Dunn-Fox from Leek

My Mum, My Hero!

Mum's there whenever I need her,
Often too at the end of the phone,
'How about going shopping dear?
Would you like a meal here at home?'

She's busy beyond all comparison,
Never sitting still for terribly long.
From where does she get all that energy?
She cycles, shops, cares, writes a song . . .

The house she looks after is huge,
There's six in our family you see,
We keep her busy with dishes piling up,
She still finds caring time for them and for me!

When she's tired and had another challenging day,
There's always more to do.
Never is there a grumble or frown,
There's encouraging words. More than a few!

Mum loves to share our happy occasions,
Passed piano exams, birthdays, weddings delight!
A proud happy smile at an offspring's success,
She's continually there, all day, all night.

Thanks mum for all you have given us,
And for all you continue to do,
You've made us strong through the fairness you've taught,
Although often unsaid, 'Mum, I love you. Thank you.'

Ruth Ironside

My Mum

Jenny Matthews is a nurse,
Looking after others with the old age curse,
Whom have lost the sanity of their minds,
And their bodies no longer function because of time,
But Jenny doesn't mind,
It's the only job she can enjoy.
And her love for the old folk really shows,
As she dresses them in their clothes,
And brushes their hair,
Then she puts them in their chair,
So they can see there's others there.
So they no longer feel alone,
Like they would if they were home.
With Jenny there, showing them care,
They will have a peaceful time,
Before they go.

Amanda Jervis

Contentment

Shed no tears now I have gone.
I loved life I had though one.
The love, the life, the tears, the sorrow -
I don't regret there is no tomorrow.

My life was full, my life was sweet.
The family circle was complete.
A wife to love, a child to care,
A heart so full there's love to spare.

The love, the joy, the tears, the sorrow,
For this was the life that I did borrow.
I hand it now for you to keep
While I lay down, to sleep, to sleep.

Hilton Joseph Holland

LINESMEN

Flick on the switch the light's not come on,
Heh! Something's amiss our electric has gone.
Phone up complain without it we're lost
Get someone out here and don't count the cost
We will there as quick as we can
I'll get in touch with our standby linesman,
A call he gets what is the time
It's just half past two and we've lost the main line,
Crawl out of bed put on some clothes,
It's still dark out and everything's froze,
No time to waste he picks up his mate
To find the right place he must make no mistake,
Ten miles they travel and three fields they walk
Tired and cold they find it hard just to talk.
For the wind is blowing and it's starting to snow
To put back the lines up the poles they must go,
Some hours have passed and the work is complete
Cold, hungry and tired they can't feel their feet.
Get home in time for the alarm to go off
So straight back to work now no time to stop,
Flick on the switch the electric's back on
About time too it's taken too long.
No thought is spared for the men who worked all night through
Bringing the warmth and light to me and to you
For they're just people we expect to be there
No matter what time they must do the repair,
So next time you reach out and switch on the light
Remember the linesman he's the light of your life.

Chris Gardner

In Memory Of A Hero

(In memory of Fire Officer Colin Townsley and the other victims who lost their lives in the Kings Cross fire 27 November 1988)

I hope that you can find a place,
Where angels never cry,
Where lovers stay together,
And flowers never die.
And the only heat upon your skin
Falls gently from the sun,
Never from a mindless deed
That someone else has done.
Though you were taken unexpectedly,
We shall not wait for your return,
For you have found a place to be
Where fires never burn.
And we have learned our lesson well,
Not to let it happen again,
Not to let your life be wasted,
Not to let you die in vain!

Tattooist Brian Nye

After You've Gone

The future was always beckoning
When we would have to part.
How could I acknowledge the reckoning
Would be the breaking of my heart.

Love true, deep and without measure
My future was always your choice
Heartfelt memories always to treasure
The emptiness no longer filled by your voice.

The bluebells will grow and bloom
And you and I will survive
The shadows creep across the room
Oh! What's the point in my being alive

We grabbed the chance to live these years.
The reckoning seemed so far away -
But here I sit alone in tears
The bill has to be paid today.

Mary Williams

I WANT

Smelly nappy
Crumpled face
Sort me out
It's a disgrace.

Feed me
Bath me
Take me out
Otherwise I'll scream and shout.

Let's go see Nanny
She'll be happy
Till she has to change a nappy.

Smile and coo
She likes a cuddle
Till she finds another puddle.

Take me home
I've had enough
I need my bed
Phew! Life's so tough.

Trevor Read

THE NURSE

What is a nurse as she wends her way
down rows of beds on a busy day
her manner is calm and her dress is white
she talks to her patients a blessed sight
she tends to the living and she
comforts the dying
she sees the smiles and she hears
the sighing
her efforts never cease when they
are in pain, her patience
dedication never in vain
she shows no fear in her
arduous task at the beck
and call of all that ask
who gives her the strength
who really knows who can say
she is flesh and blood there is
no doubt but there's more
to this nurse as she glides about
she looks to the Lord at the end
of the day knowing He'll guide
her along the way
so what is a nurse? I hear
you ask dedicated to
this special task
the answer is simple the
message is clear
she's an angel of mercy
so have no fear
her strength is there for all to see
sanctioned from above
her courage and her faith inspired by His love.

Barbara Wycherley

HAPPINESS!

A chuckling babe in mother's arms,
Where else will we find such charms?
True joyousness free from alarms
True bond of happiness, without qualms!

Even the simplest little gift
From a sad face will often shift
Deep gloom and a smile will lift
Into shining eyes - a change so swift!

In a world of so much sadness
Let us ever be alert for gladness;
Though not one of us is sinless,
Let us not suffer from too much dimness!

Do we smile when we meet our neighbours
And pay due respect to the one who labours
Night and day not looking for favours,
With a kind word and a smile, for such he savours!

A kindly word with honesty fraught
Will often reduce sadness to naught
And lift one's spirits, however, taut,
To some sublime region, the Heavenly sort!

Many will find happiness even when alone;
Others need companionship to revive their own
Happy thoughts, while many still need to be shown
The multitudinous ways in which happiness can atone!

Claude Knight

The Carers

The doctors, white coats, open and flapping
rush to the aid of a person in need,
the hours that they work, would leave many lacking
but for the dedication, and willpower of steel.

Their job is certainly not always a happy one,
for some there is hope, for others there is none,
there is bad news to give, this you cannot ignore
sometimes you wish you could be swallowed by the floor.

The wonder of a baby born into the world
eyes closed tight, and fingers all curled,
the pleasure of new parents, the love they portray
this and this alone, helps get them through the day.

Broken bones, bloody noses, all to be seen
washing and sterilising, every wound until clean.
A bleeper goes off, someone ill on the ward.
Rushing down corridors, never time to get bored.

What is a nine to five job, this they have never had.
What is sleep, of this, many times they would be glad.
Their unending dedication, could put us to shame,
to them this is the survival for life, not a joke or a game.

C Flory

Unsung Heroes

You enlighten me
In your solitude
I watch you
In my interlude.

You're always calm
Thoughtful and bright
Anyone's pleasure in the light
You enhance my appetite

You do things
That nobody would think of
Many would spread it about
And pretend to be boss

So you're my hero
To the handicapped downtrodden and old
You make a sacrifice
You have a place in my soul.

Catherine McAloon

SHAYNE

Three weeks ago in November,
        When I was fast asleep,
My grandson phoned me from London
        With news he couldn't keep.

His wife had given birth, to his second son,
        And as excited dads always do,
He had to phone everybody,
        Tho' it was only half-past two.

He is my second great-grandson,
        And I am proud to say,
I'm looking forward to seeing him,
        Though they live so far away.

A baby girl was to be named *Sheila* after Gran,
        Or maybe my name, which is *Jane.*
So for a boy, it was parts of both names,
        'Cos they named the baby Shayne.

Jean Hendrie

SOLDIERS OF NATURE

They work and drink and fight this breed
to death and danger pay no heed
with pride each man he stands in line
the unnamed heroes of our time
their quest to see the eagle fly
in its kingdom high of sky
to see the lion walking free
to love the whale and let it be
they ease the fall of Mother Nature
and make her glory even greater
the sleepless nights the endless days
to their kind none sing their praise
they carry scars some deep and raw
some give their life by tiger's paw
their tears and blood they give with pride
their heads held high on nature's side
the broken hearts on seeing death
the joy of helping life's first breath
aching arms at end of day
reward of heart their only pay
strength of heart guides them every one
untiring labour never done
to living glory they make their stand
to keep this earth as nature planned
they give their lives to living kind
these unnamed heroes of our time.

Terry Bobrowicz

TAMLYN

Lee, Kelly the words that I hear
The pattering feet are getting near
The stairs the first challenge to overcome
Will she succeed or fall on her bum?

She clambers up as fast as a rabbit
Kicks in the door like kicking a bad habit
She comes running in and says, I want a drink,
But it spills on my carpet that starts to stink.

She spies a bag of crisps from her eye
When she goes go get them I have to lie
There's none left, I put them out of sight
But she'll get them, I know she might.

She goes to the stereo and says music on
Then tells me to dance to her favourite song
But I beg, no, no, no, Uncle Lee is tired
And from now on in her eyes I'm no longer admired.

She goes over to Kelly and says, jumpy, jumpy
But if you fall off Lee's bed you'll go bumpy, bumpy
So she jumps to the ground and says, round and round
But Uncle Lee ends up lying on the ground.

Another day is over which has been rather racy
She'll soon be going home with her mummy Tracey,
Tracey, good luck the words that I say
Because there's another one due in May.

Lee Broadrick

Swahili?

Oh no! She's going to give it to me!
Her little bundle of joy was sitting on my knee!
I tried to do all the things people should, I bounced it up and down
'til it threw up on her Chinese silk rug!
Politely but firmly she regained her self-control, sneering
'So strange?'
I just felt complete relief, I'd rather handle a dog with mange!
She oooohed at it, she aaaahed a bit, she rocked it with ne'er a blink,
Then took our one of her 40 double D's 'He needs a little drink!'
I looked at the ceiling, the windows then the floor as it
glug glugged away
And she got out the other one, as a sort of encore!
She spoke to it in an alien tongue, it responded and appeared
quite happy,
Just a as I bit into my chocolate bun she beamed
'He's done a nappy!'
Without more ado she spread-eagled it to the ground!
Searching in her voluminous holdall not a baby wipe to be found!
This dialogue only known to them went on throughout
the botty cleaning
'Who's a ickly uvvy baby den?' It looked up at her hoop
earrings, gleaming!
I'd abandoned the chocolate cake, sipped my coffee double quick,
Until now I'd never believed there could be anything worse
than cat sick!
Was there something wrong with me?
I began to have serious doubts as to my instincts, my femininity!
There must be a missing link in my heredity!
On leaving this pantomime disguised as a charity coffee morning,
I went there for a good cause, a lamb to the slaughter without
fair warning!
I asked my pal, 'Is there something wrong with me?'
She replied with a smile, 'No love I'm the same we'll be fine
once we've
Got used to the idea, and of course when we can speak . . . Swahili!'

At last in the quiet of my own little flat I sip my wine and
stroke the cat,
Turn on the telly, curl up in my 'jarmies' sit cross-legged on the mat,
Look down at my 32A's and give them a reassuring little pat!
I'll not learn Swahili, and that's safely that!

Joyce M Hefti-Whitney

I'M CONFUSED

I am a bouncin' baby boy, just arrived on planet Earth,
To find I share the leading role, with someone giving birth.
Strange things happen at this time, in the delivery ward,
I'm all geared up to bungi jump, till someone cut the cord.

So many things are going on; 'It's a boy' they all sigh,
Then grab me by my tiny feet, and smack me till I cry,
That's no way to treat a baby, I mean, I wasn't even late,
This all happened long before they bothered to check my weight.

Next they had a poke around, seeing if all my bits were there,
Checking every nook-n-cranny, then washed and brushed my hair,
They dressed me in a nightie, and wrapped me in a woolly shawl,
Stuffing me with loads of milk, each time I start to bawl.

Menu options don't exist, milk is the one and only choice,
The trouble is they give it me, each time I air my voice,
But I do get my own back, and for sure they're none too happy,
If in the middle of the night, I really fill my nappy.

Another thing I noticed, after taking milk squirt after squirt,
I'm thrown upon a shoulder, and hit on my back until I burp,
'Coochy coo well done' they say, as I belch and pass my wind,
If my big bruvver does the same, he's chastised 'cos he's sinned.

Wenn the Pen

Nephews Are A Nuisance . . . But Nice!

My two nephews
Are like sugar and spice;
One is awful,
One is nice.

Michael is two,
He *looks* chubby and cute,
But looks are deceptive
And so is that brute!

My two nephews
Josh and Mike
One is lovely
One's a tyke!

Josh is six months,
All blonde and giggly
Blue-eyed staring
Plump and wriggly.

Even though it's tough,
I'd swear an oath
That though it's hard,
I love them both!

Lynda Blagg

Aet R.I.P.

Angela is dead and gone,
And, though it isn't funny,
She didn't amount to very much
But she didn't half spend some money.

Her family will miss her.
Of that there is no doubt.
She wasn't much of a mother
But she sure could flippin' shout.

So don't put flowers on her grave,
Don't cry all over it.
Just give to her what she deserves
And trample her a bit.

Angela Tomlinson

KILLING REGRET

Why is it that on the brightest day
the hounds of hell can spring in my way
with all my mistakes of the past?
They torment me until, at last,
survival instinct rescues me.
Switch on the radio, hear a voice.
Don't care what, I have no choice.
Anything to stop the pain I feel
when thoughts make it all so real
again - curse my memory.
They can't make a drug that kills regret.
I know that you have forgiven me, and yet
until I can forgive myself, and leave
the past where it lies and cease to grieve;
I know there is no hope for me.

Gillian Avis

Night Feed

Down of hair, dimpled cheeks
Tiny hands tiny feet
He sleeps

Puckered brow, gives out a yell
To toss and turn
As hunger prevails
He wakes

Bottle feed nappy change
Cuddled well
Laid back down
To sleep again

Mother sighs goes back to bed
Hoping now
To get some rest
Till morning light.

Doreen Warren

You

You made the storm blow over,
The sun begin to shine,
A very special person,
I wish you could be mine.

I will never hurt you,
You will never need to cry,
My love will last forever,
Yours till the day I die.

Dave Maxfield

TEARS

Tears of sadness and tears of joy
Tears that are falling for my little boy
My eyes are o'erflowing but what can I do
To make you aware of my love for you?

Your hands are so tiny your eyes are so blue
Your hair is like silk your skin is brand new
What have I done in bringing you here
To a world without love and one filled with fear?

How can I shelter one so tender and dear
From the hate of mankind in another new year?
Where there's no shelter for our children tho' oh so young
And who will then care when the last song is sung?

You arrived like an angel to a world full of sin
And I opened my heart and let you come in
With your heart and your soul so full of trust
I gave you a world full of hate and of lust

All that I have is a few very short years
To save you from harm and all of the tears
Then you'll be a man and live your own life
To start over again with your very own wife

Until then my dear son I will be by your side
I won't tell you lies or e'en try to hide
The truth from your eyes nor from your ears
Tho' it will be painful over the years

And yes once again my eyes fill with tears
When I hear the sweet sound of your voice in my ears
So don't be afraid my beautiful son
To cry for a world of which you are one

Fiona Higgins

INSIDE

The babe cried,
Warmly wrapped within,
To me it's tied,
It's surely screamin',
Let me grow!
Time to air
My feelings so!
I'll kick as hard as I dare
Beating my fists
I'll tug and twist
Around my wrists
Soon I pray
You'll hear me
And then you may be
Able to set me free
What's out there
That you try to hide?
I know you care
But I must confide
I'm longing to explore
Beyond the warmth I'm hidden in
There must be more beyond the secret door
To livin'.

Nicola Linfield

GRAVE WORDS

I am a hypochondriac
A hypochondriac am I
What words will be put
On my stone when I die.

They'll say I was a moaner
Full of woe and gloom
Glad to be rid of me
When I'm in my tomb.

But I know what I'd put
That's if I had my pick
I'd write upon my stone
'Now do you believe I'm sick?'

David Brownley

My Departure

When my life comes to an end
Money I don't want people to spend
I don't want anyone to feel sad
A better life I couldn't have had
I didn't happen to win the Lottery
So my ashes will rest in unglazed pottery
In my life I learnt a lot
And am gracious and thankful for what I've got
Brothers and sisters abound galore
Younger life for me was never a bore
We had many good hidings, many a cane
But came back for more forgetting the pain
Mind, life for me wasn't too unkind
I always had plenty to fill my mind
It was knitting, sewing, writing you name it
My active mind was a bottomless pit
When I hopefully get to the vast heavens above
I'll be watching you all and surround you with love.

Cicley Cockwell

UNTITLED

We once were together but now you are gone,
Although I still worship the ground you walk on,
You hate me, I love you, it's a one-sided thing,
Forever I'll love you so I'll keep trying,
I've asked you out, you said I don't know,
Eventually your answer will be no.
You've done it before I guess I just do not learn,
To be held in your arms again I yearn.
If a miracle could happen and my dreams come true,
All I'd want is to be loved by you.
I can't get you out of my head,
I dream of you when I'm in bed,
I'm crazy about you,
Do you feel that way too?
I dream of us together,
We'd fall out never,
You hold my hand and flirt you see,
Don't you realise what that does to me?
If you showed your feelings maybe we'd be together once more,
And mend my heart which you once tore,
That would never happen 'cos you hate me so much,
To kiss you and hold you or even to touch,
Forget him, people say, easier said than done,
If you love me again we could have lots of fun.

Laura Kingswood (14)

So Much To Say

'Did you see Martha or was it Jane
Holding hands with Thomas
Down St David's Lane?
I went to the shops
Guess who I saw?
No, not cousin Molly!
Let me tell you more . . .
When I stripped the settee
Guess what I found?
Not that sock you lost
An old half a crown!
I went to Mrs Hughes
And had a cup of tea
She told me
About Peter the post
Oh! Dearie me!
By the way
Did you have a good day?'

This will be my epitaph . . .
She had so much to say!

G M Thomas

Stalled

Without you I'm empty,
No petrol, no fuel,
My engine won't start,
The brakes are on full.

Pain punctures my tyres,
Releasing all air,
This body has nothing,
Without you there.

Julie McKerchar

DAD

Always there to comfort me
A soft and gentle man
You always know just what I need
You help me if you can
You never moan complaints are few
But deep inside you're hurting too
You keep it in you won't let go
The pain you feel, you never show
You hide it to protect us all
A man you stand, you never fall
You've cared for me, I love you so
I never want to let you go
You're strong although you're fading fast
You're all for the future
Never the past
Always for others in your mind
A lovely man your heart so kind
And now you've got to go away
Your time has come you cannot stay
But if I had one wish come true
I'd wish that I could be with you
When you're no longer here with me
I'll miss you until eternity
The gentle smile, the friendly face
No one will ever take your place
I love you Dad.

Vanessa Ball

Parental Training College

Why is it your parents can't help nagging you,
Maybe it's what they've been trained to do?
You get in from school and it's 'Why are you late?'
'The bus didn't come so I had to wait.'

The next morning it's close to all-out war,
My parents are both so hard to ignore,
I reckon there's a college where parents go,
Where they learn how to nag, annoy and say 'No!'

When you ask to go out the answer is 'Where?'
I don't even think that they really care,
Do you think that they learnt at a special place,
And they learn how to deal with every case?

When I'm a parent I won't do that,
I'll offer 'em sweets and make them fat!
I'll skip classes at that training place,
And I won't dress my children in pretty lace.

When I'm a parent, I'll be really nice,
When they ask to go out, I won't think twice,
When I'm a parent, I won't lay down any laws,
When I'm a parent, I'll ignore all the chores!

Danielle Morey (14)

My Epitaph

Here lies me
Peacefully
I lived a long life
With not a moment of strife
And died of BSE

Omaira Gill

ODE TO THE BARD

Handsome raffin excise lad
Wi' the darkest deevilish e'en
Rabbie - ye rule in Scotland
The best - that's iver been

Poetry - it knew fortune
Nae langer - wis it blurred
For - mony a hert - it gleddened
An' mony - it also spurred

Ma distant dream - dear Rabbie
Is tae be - a bit like you
Oh! Rabbie Burns - the wunner
Yer banter - inspires - an' woos

An' if this nicht -
God bless ye
Ye are in some 'higher' sphere
Whaur the licht - is bricht an' shinin'
Look fondly -doon by here

See me! - a learnin' poet
Though no' a maister -
Shair - a fan
Wha' wid dedicate - this sonnet
Tae Rabbie Burns -
The Bard - an' man.

Irene Gunnion

When I'm Gone

When I'm gone you will remember me,
You will miss me lots just wait and see,
You will sit alone and start to cry,
You won't forget me no matter how hard you try,
You better start getting yourself prepared,
For when you remember the good times we shared,
Every day you will sing my song,
That's when you realise I was right all along,
Forgetting me will be tough,
You will want me back soon enough,
Unfortunately then it will be too late,
Maybe you will just put it down to fate,
You will wish I was standing in sight,
When you remember me in the dark night,
After a while maybe you won't remember me well,
But that's something only time will tell.

Simha Taj

Cheers

Her glass was full of lager
Her dreams were of George Best
Her motto '*In a minute*'
But now she's laid to rest.

No more half-hearted diets
We miss her lots and lots
The best excuse she's ever had
For leaving the dirty pots!

Corinne England

Quick! Hide The Welcome Mat!

You've probably met the type before -
The moment they walk in the door
Their eyes are going everywhere.
You show them politely to a chair
Then find they've followed to the kitchen,
Where you're making coffee and they're itching
To inspect every little cranny and nook,
Nothing escapes their hawk-like look.
They are experts at *damning with faint praise*
And one of their less endearing ways
Is to say in tones that drip with ice,
'Oh yes - it really looks *quite* nice.'
While all the time they chatter madly
About their *friends,* and how badly
Their health has been - how they suffer!
No-one ever has had life rougher,
And battle, murder and sudden death
Whilst scarcely pausing to draw breath.
Why do they think that they're the one
To advise on how things *should* be done?
I feel that murder and sudden death will be
Theirs - and it will be done by me!

Joan Weston

See You In A While

He went quite suddenly, my friend Bill,
He wasn't that old and hadn't been ill.
Still I can see him say, with a smile:
'OK then, see you in a while.'

I waved to the others and said goodbye,
And as I didn't know he was going to die
And because it was six and getting late
I didn't turn back when I got to the gate.

Imagine my feelings when the next day
A friend rang to say he had just passed away.
I know we shall meet up again when I die,
But I wish I had gone back to bid him goodbye.

Now all this has made me think a good deal
About death and life and the emotions we feel
When loved ones pass over without a farewell.
So 'Act as you're prompted' is the moral I tell.

Elizabeth Riches

Memories Of Nicholas (Nick)

Dear Nick so many times I think of you and cry
Why at so young an age did you have to die?
I think back over the years, the happy times we shared
I think of the work you did for others, how you cared
I try to be happy, but so often I'm blue
The reason being I cannot stop thinking of you!
Whenever I see geese flying in the sky
I think of you Nick and again I cry

You were so full of life, to be with, such fun
A dearly loved brother, a caring son
Your love of the Arts, and nature too
Happy and lovely dreams I have of you
Your wonderful smile, your eyes so blue

We will always remember you with love and pride
Your endless works for charities, you took in your stride
We know you would wish us to be happy not sad
You are in a better place Nick so we must be glad!
You were so very talented and so very clever
But Nick in our hearts you will live for *ever!*

Elaine M Jordan

THE COMPUTER HAS ASSUMED TOO MUCH . . .

I'm a microchip computer with an electronic mind:
I'm held in very high regard tho' sometimes much maligned;
No wonder I'm deflated - my performance underrated -
A sophisticate intelligence not of the human kind.

I'm a microchip computer with an automatic brain:
I'm fed with the wrong data but it's me that takes the blame;
My intellect's insuperable, my memory indisputable -
A master-mind, created from a scientific dream.

I'm a microchip computer, I was born without a soul,
I hear you're working on it but you won't achieve this goal:
Fashioned from technology - I can't *do* sociology -
Personal relations does not fall within my role.

I'm a microchip computer and your wish is my command,
And tho' I'll do my best for you, to meet all your demands,
Questions in profusion only lead to my confusion;
Please be more specific or you'll surely blow my mind.

I'm a microchip computer but I cannot stand the pace:
It was never my desire to join this world's atomic chase;
So when you finally press my key don't stare with incredulity -
It was not my decision to destroy the human race.

Cynthia M Oliver

AFTER I'VE GONE

After I've gone
you'll find there's a space
at tables, in bed,
which used t'be my place.

It won't be for long
you'll put something else there
move the furniture round,
give someone my chair.

Then you'll forget
As life slowly moves on
It'll all settle down again
After I've gone.

Anne Clegg

WHEN I'M GONE

Is this the end or a new beginning
        Am I a loser or am I winning
I tried my best, or nearly so
        In the end I had to let go.

So goodbye world now what for
        Will I go through that special door
Or just rest as in a sleep
        No more pains, no bones to creak.

If spiritual life is as a beautiful dream
        I'll be happy to join the scene
So think of me with happiness
        For life is a trial at its best.

My body now is obsolete
        With my wings I'm now complete
I'm flying with the birds and bees
        Feeling happy and at ease.

If questions keep coming to your mind
        The answers you will never find
Till you come over to the other side
        And with me as a spirit reside.

Gladys C'Ailceta

THANK GOD

You have always been here,
You have always been dear,
A life built with you ever near
Not a thought have I given,
To the future days, how I'd feel
When you are gone,
This is not so clear.
It comes to everyone, one day
A sad sad parting along the way
Enjoy the precious moments while we can
For tomorrow you may not be here to stay . . .
Let me hold you close and hold your
tiny hand,
As you are all I have
And thank God
For all the joys you bring.

Liz Dicken

APROPOS

Never liked
The metric way -
So on this
My final day,
Out with metrics
Now I pray -
Two yards down
Is where I'll stay!

Gerald Whitehouse

Goodbye Dear Friend

Beneath the ground lies a dear friend
Who kept us laughing up to the end.
Life to her was one big joke
And her humour spread
To other folk.

Never a dull moment
Was had with Sue
For when passing a compliment
She'd unwittingly insult you!

She loved her 'grub' - there is no doubt
And wouldn't let anyone
Throw anything out
A sandwich here - a cream cake there
Pasties and scones
She didn't care.

Nothing ever went in the bin
Yet despite all that
She still stayed slim.
Even as she lay
Ill and dying
Everyone around was laughing
Not crying
At the last few words
She uttered -
'I'd love a slice of toast
Lightly buttered.'
Alas now this dear friend is gone
But laughter and memories linger on.

Susan Long

Here He Lies

They wrote this on my
Tombstone
When they said 'Now he
is gone!'
They planted flowers
Upon the grave, as they
Sang a 'parting song':

Now little do they wonder,
Little do they know;
I'm not gone up 'yonder'
or yet gone down below!
I'm waiting here beside
them
But I've nothing now to show.

The body I had my life in,
Like a bottle full of beer,
Got smashed upon the roadside,
But there is no cause to fear,
I've found another bottle;
I filled this bottle up again,
Now, once again I'm here!

George Ponting

THERE IS NO JUSTICE

At first she felt guilty
for leaving him.
Now she can really see,
he was no good and never would be.

He never gave love, so why does he bicker,
only saw her as a mother figure.
Anything in his path he'd shatter,
his only aim was climbing up the ladder.

With his selfish mind,
He took revenge on the child.
How that child sobbed and wept,
Over the promises he never kept.

He's shown his true colours,
playing his trump card so well.
Now she has a living hell,
the child is hurting and in pain,
Why should he care, he has no shame.

Oh yes things are as clear as mud,
He's turned his back,
On his own flesh and blood.

Does the devil really look after his own,
Because all the love and respect
of that child he owns.
It's ironic but sadly true,
She's the loser.
From where I stand it should be you.

Antoinette Spooner

MENOPAUSE

Is it really hot in here
or is it just my age?
How long before I am through
this menopausal stage?

I've always been nice and slim
size 12 would fit just right.
I started going through my change
became a 16 overnight.

I seem to get in such a state
one minute happy next I'm sad.
Do you have to look at me that way,
you're driving me quite mad.

My husband tries to understand
when for no reason I start to yell.
And throw whatever comes to hand,
he's learnt to dodge them well.

Your menopause isn't any worse
than adolescence or so we're told.
I looked forward to becoming a woman, though
I'm dreading getting *old.*

Kim Bettley

MY VALENTINE GIRL

Hair of gold and eyes of green
The prettiest girl I've ever seen
Your smile is like a summer's day
And brighter than the month of May

So lithe in movement, young and free
You're fairer than the world to me
A field of flowers can't compete
The fairest bloom is hard to beat

This loving heart I give to you
If I lost your love I would be blue
You light my day and light my life
So please my darling be my wife

When time passes and you're old and grey
I will love you as I do today
You'll always be my Valentine girl
More lovely than the rarest pearl

Barbara Kern

My Life

I never asked a lot from life,
A home, a family, a loving wife.
Happiness, contentment, a comfy chair,
Food on the table, crisp clean air.
A job to do, a place to sleep!
A decent wage, my family to keep.
A place in society, the rat race won;
To go, now and then, to a place in the sun.
Cosy winter nights, sat round the fire
Perhaps now and then, a video on hire!
To watch the children play on the floor,
Brisk autumn walks along the seashore.
To see the fishing boats, coming and going,
To take part in life's to-ing and fro-ing.
And when I look at what I have got
I think to myself! Not a bad little lot.
When the time comes for me to depart,
I'll know I did alright! Deep down in my heart!

Richard Ninnis

A Mother's Fond Remembrance

My little girl of only three
Sadly departed for eternity
Her short blonde hair cut in a fringe
She wasn't one to moan or whinge
Her lovely smile on cheery days
Lit our lives a hundred ways
Her eyes of blue sparkled and shone
But now alas she's sadly gone
She left her mark where'er she went
Full of mischief she was hell bent
Her brother she tried to get into trouble
And lived her short life at the double
I'm sure she knew she hadn't long
On earth to dwell and to us belong
Alas to heaven she quickly went
To us below she was only lent.

In three short years we loved her dearly
We think about her, not just yearly
But as at last we're getting older
I long to hug and tenderly hold her
I know one day we'll meet again
But for now I don't know when.

Marion Pollitt

The Night We Fell In Love

You looked at me across the room
And all my thoughts began to bloom
You came and asked me if I'd dance
I knew at once we had a chance.

We danced and danced the whole night through
I looked into your eyes of blue
I saw such kindness, care and love
And thanked the stars that shone above.

You walked me home to my front door
I never could have asked for more
I'd found someone to love and trust
Be true to you, I know I must.

Today we're married and you are mine
So please say you're my Valentine
For as long as the sun shines in the sky
I'll love you till the day I die.

Joanne Davison

LIFE WITHIN A LIFE

A child is born of man and woman's seed.
At the time of its birth it does not know pain.
It does not know greed.
It is as fragile as a piece of glass.
Its innocence for long won't last.
It has only the future it has no past.
The time of its birth its stars were cast.
What its future holds is in the heavens.
What its dislikes and likes are.
Will it get to be famous or get to go far.
Will it be rich or will it be poor
What will its colour be black or white.
Will it be a coward or learn to fight.
A child is a child no matter what.
It doesn't matter how much money its parents
Have got.
It may be white as snow or black as coal.
But when it's born it has one goal.
To become the person planted in its soul.

Valerie Wood

Graduation Day

Your graduation's here at last
And, though exams are long since past,
Today's the day we sing out loud,
Congratulations! We're so proud
Of everything that you've achieved,
For, through the years we've watched you weave
This tapestry, which is your life,
And though you may find threads of strife,
They're oversewn with treasured pearls
So, when your tapestry's unfurled
You only see the happy days,
Embroidered in a golden haze.
Feel proud as you don cap and gown,
You're now a person of renown!
As your diploma you collect,
Upon the years you will reflect -
You've worked so hard to reach your goal,
Now there's contentment in your soul;
The many special days you've shared
With people who have really cared.
And may today be special too,
No-one deserves it more than you.

Kay Spurr

Love Wars

Love is like a battle, the war inside fights on,
There is no kind of armour, it can protect you from,
It pierces through, any metal, it clutches at your heart,
Once it's got you hooked, it's very hard to part.

It can last a day, and sometimes even a year,
Or maybe even a lifetime, so special, so dear,
The feelings you have, the warmth inside,
There's nothing to fear, and nothing to hide.

The stage is set, the dreams begin,
He's your special person, and you want to be with him,
Day and night, your thoughts divide,
You must let your heart be your guide.

A rose, the sign of the love between you,
Red to say, forever true,
The wonderful times, that are yet to share,
Three simple words show you care.

Dianne Brown

13.3.96

Such devastation hit Dunblane.
The suffering the tears, the pain.
The madman, killing innocents.
Yet no-one knew of his intents.
He came inside Dunblane's school gym,
He had many guns with him,
Shot at teachers and the class,
And left behind a bloody mass
The mothers heard of the affair
Rushed to see, was their child there?
In anguish, waiting to be told
If it was their child, lying cold.
Despair and wailing in the places,
The worried looks upon their faces.
No-one could hold back the tears
When hearing of the worst of fears.
Sixteen, five-year-olds, were slain.
The gunman had nothing to gain.
A teacher shot, and then him too.
As to why! There's not a clue.

Margaret Rankin

MOTHER AND CHILD

Right at the start of your birth
I knew you'd make your mark on earth
From the moment I held you in my arms
I was aware of all your charms
It was obvious for all the world to see
That you were precious and special to me.

I nurtured you and watched you grow
But there comes a time when a mum should know
Their child has to go their own way
Discover their future and have their own say
Like a butterfly emerging with wings unfurled
You took your own place in this world.

After you gained an education, and all the rest
I was left with my empty nest
But although in distance we are apart
You've left sweet memories in my heart.

Denise Broad

JUST THINKING YOUR NAME

Sweet memories of you, help me through the night
Knowing you're with me, makes everything right
Just thinking your name, just knowing you're near
Someone so special, our future so clear.

Not alone do I feel, when I think of you
Love and affection, in all that you do
I feel your strong arms, your warm embrace
Your tender touch, exploring my face.

When I dream of you, passion, ignites fire
Flames so wild, burning higher and higher
Desire so strong, words just cannot say
Love so intense, like the breaking of day.

Though we're not together
We're never apart
Because now and forever
You're held in my heart.

S J Eley

How Do You Know You're Here?

How do you know you're here my friend?
Perhaps you're really not!
No-one's ever proved we are,
No-one's proved we're not.
From the oldest inhabitant,
To the kiddy in the cot,
No-one knows the answer,
When, why, what;
No-one knows the answer,
I doubt they ever will,
The question's a disturbing one,
I fear the answer's more disturbing still?
Time may give us the answer.
As the years go by,
Of how we came to be here,
If we are, and why!

Brian Slade

THE RING OF CONFIDENCE

You need confidence to grow in the womb -
When to know it's time to arrive
And make that hard journey into the world -
Win the struggle involved to survive.

You need confidence for that first big smile
And to focus at last on your mum.
Then to sit up and crawl - learn to play,
What a comfort is that special thumb!

You need confidence for that first school day -
Face the shock that you've left mum at home,
But it's not too long 'fore you're big and strong
Reaching teenage when childhood has flown.

You need confidence now my precious son
As to manhood you rapidly grow,
The world to conquer - it offers you much
But remember you reap what you sow.

You need confidence as the years slip by
With many pitfalls to overcome -
But love and joy join the circle of life
Before you sleep with the setting sun.

Paddy Jupp

POMP AND CIRCUMSTANCE

Strutting like a prize peacock
He makes his presence felt
His entourage assume it's dead-lock
In whose mouth butter wouldn't melt.

The hangers on wait on his every word
As if it had been sculptured by hand
He is as far as they are concerned a lord
When he oversees his land.

Honesty and integrity are his bread and butter
Although some around are heard to mutter
Subversives are not playing cricket
More than likely they'll be pickets

Reality dramatically appears
And with it all those unfounded fears
Sober as a judge
Left with no issues to fudge
Homeward safely they all trudge.

Alistair Buchanan

PORTFOLIO

Life can be a daunting track
As there is no turning back
When you go it alone
And realise you're on your own.
An unknown result
From child to adult
Experience in nothing
Each day for learning.
The interviews you attend
Your occupation, money to spend
All the miles you roam
Before finding your first home.
Romance knocks on your door
A risk to take you're unsure
Your future planned and neat
The wedding bells, new heartbeat.
Suddenly becoming a widow
Watching the child grow
The older years crept along
You came, but now you're gone.

Karen Cook

WINTER: DELIGHT OF YOUTH, DREAD OF AGE

Wake in the morning,
Snow is falling,
The world is white,
A child's delight.
Sledges sliding,
Snowballs flying.
A snowman grows
With carrot nose
And woollen scarf.
Children laugh,
Their faces glow,
Enjoying the snow.

Frail and old,
Hating the cold,
The winter chill
Makes her ill.
She draws her chair
Nearer the fire
And pulls her wrap
Over her lap.
Afraid to go
Out in the snow
Lest she slip and fall.
Her room is her jail
The winter through,
A dismal view.
Can she believe
She will survive?

Anne Crofton Dearle

Yesterday, Today, Tomorrow

Yesterday,
I could play all night,
And next day still feel fine.
I could dance and party,
And have a ball,
And for my bed, not pine.

Paradoxically,
Life was oh, so serious;
I thought I had the answers to it all.
Although I was so young,
I would have felt so stung,
If anyone had called me a young fool!

Now, today,
I get very weary,
And need eight hours' sleep.
I sit in silence,
Let others have fun,
Whilst off to bed I creep.

Along the way,
I've learned I *know* nothing,
There's nothing of which I feel certain.
I see things more clearly,
I'm happier, really,
Not seeing life through youth's net curtain.

Tomorrow,
Is just another day.
For its coming I can calmly wait.
Lost certainty of youth,
And doubting what is *truth*,
Takes away the urge to speculate.

David South

PAST YEARS

The first thing I remember is the softness of her skin,
A gentle voice a warm sweet smell a safeness felt within,
As years went by the family grew a sister and two brothers
The fun we had in growing up the love we showed each other,
In summer days at Cayton Bay the sunshine and the sea,
These memories are so precious they mean so much to me,
As time went on I fell in love which was then to change my life,
So down the aisle on my dad's arm as I became a wife,
Our children brought such joy to us four daughters and a son,
Such happy times as they grew up so many days of fun.
Our Christmases were special the best we ever had,
The children playing football, trying to catch their dad,
Then sad times as they left home and went their separate ways,
An empty house can seem so cold and longer are your days,
Now time to find the love we shared when there was just we two,
It seems so many years ago to when our love was new.
And so we grew much closer a time for us to share,
We did the things we wanted, we lived without a care.
Our children had their children and we played a different role,
Now grandad could not run so fast as he always stood in goal.
Our bones became much weaker and our eyesight faded fast,
But the memories of my life in my heart forever last.

Julie Staff

LOST LOVE

Emotional was the feeling
On the Last Night of the Proms.
The wine, the mood, the music
Are now distant and all gone.

I'll never forget our parting
It was filled with such deep sorrow;
I never wanted it to end,
I needed a tomorrow.

Yesterdays are treasured,
But todays are torn apart.
I only hope the future
Can mend this broken heart.

The love we had and the love we shared
Should have been forever.
Now all I have are memories
Of our joyous times together.

Sylvia Higgins

TIME PASSING

If I could sail on one more tide
Or climb another mountainside
The joy of youth I would know again
And still be striving to attain
Fulfilment of the impossible dream
All earth's wonders to have seen

Southern sea and silver shore
Rugged headland rocky tor
Calling me to explore
Just one more time just one time more.

Deep the yearning and the longing
Sad the knowing time has gone,
Fireside slippers now for me
Easy chair and memory.

Goodbye to mountain's furrowed face
Goodbye to nature's wild embrace
For time the healer, time the stealer
Is time the winner of the race.

Margaret B Copeman

MEMORIES

I visit here often,
Get the strength from the trees,
And a lifetime of memories
Ride with the breeze.
The warmth of the sun
The heart to uplift,
The fragrance of flowers
Truly a gift.
The song of the birds
As they glide through the air.
Our children at play
Without worry or care.
Your red, rosy lips,
The warmth of your smile.
Wish you'd sit down beside me
And talk for a while.
I miss you so much
I have shed many tears,
Although you've been gone
For so many years.
I am old, and I'm weak now
And dim is my light,
And we'll soon be together
I know my end is in sight.
I've almost finished my journey
Through the cycle of life.
Then my wish will be granted -
I'll be with you, dear wife.

Susie Mehmed

WITH ACHING HEART

I wandered lonely on the beach
For love, my love was out of reach.
No matching footprints; no warm hand
But endless sea and endless sand.

Just yesterday I knew love's kiss,
Not desolation such as this.
Love's gentle ripples were no more,
Just large waves pounding on the shore.

Dear love. In you I felt complete.
With you the air was always sweet.
Each day was warm and oh so still.
I shivered in the breeze's chill.

I felt the peace would never die.
Love only knew the bluest sky.
It filled with joy my heart and soul.
In love I felt content and whole.

Love only knew the brightest flowers.
In love I spent such happy hours.
Love only knew each bird's pure song
And in its power the weak were strong.

Love only knew a way to share
And taught each heart to deeply care.
Love gentle; perfect; love so kind
Why did you go and leave me blind.

Dear love. This parting hurts so much.
I need the comfort of your touch.
With aching heart I stand and cry
That in your arms once more I'll lie.

John Christopher

Love In The Nineties

We're living off the DSS
my girlfriend Kate and me.
We have an under-heated flat
Our cat for company.

It's not as if I *wouldn't* work,
- the baby's due in May.
I've tried and tried to find a job
- whatever some folk say.

I love my Kate with all my heart.
She's warm and kind and clever.
She made the woolly knitted quilt
We use in wintry weather.

I've put up shelves just for her use.
We got, from here and there,
All sorts of useful furniture
And Kate's old rocking chair.

Our flat is in the basement
and sometimes rather damp,
But when the night is drawing in
and Kate turns on the lamp

She says it's like a cosy cave
With cushions on the floor.
That's where we sit, wrapped in
our quilt
I couldn't ask for more.

Except perhaps, not long from now
A job, so that I can
Stop worrying. Become at last
A self-reliant man.

Ann F Rudy

Inspired By Love

My inspiration, comes from you
I breathe for you, alone
You're everything, that's good in life
Life's trials, you atone

I marvel, at the moon and stars
The sun, the wind and rain
The beauty that surrounds me
I've come alive again

The reasons that I see, are clear
God's gift, to me is you
You've brought me hope, and happiness
And love, so strong and true

Within your arms, I'm not afraid
As safe, I'll always be
And in your eyes, I see for sure
Your only love, is me

The future now, is truly sealed
For you and I to share
Within each other's shadow
As lovers so declare

This love so deep, and meaningful
Will guide us through the years
And help us face, what world will bring
Dispelling all our fears

And even when, such life does fade
And either left to grieve
In life, in love, not one regret
Except, this world to leave

Roy Wyatt

HONEYCOMBED

Layers of frothy petticoats
Rounded out
beneath a full-skirted Linzi dress a-flouncing
Dolcis winkle-picker
stepping feet
I'm toe-pinched ready for the dancing
Bouffant hairstyle
beehive fashion
teased from silken tresses flowing
lacquered a-la-pompadour fragrant
in perfumed clouds of Blue Grass scent
my face creme-puffed and glowing
All set for jazz club jiving
Coffee bar hiving
Smooching to RCA records of Elvis Presley
he of the lips
swivel hips
Rockin'n'rolling - kingly he impressed me.
Fluttering petty notes
scattered out
fragrant leaves of salad-days - girlish fun romancing
Brownie-box snapshots
slipper my feet
toes pinch at the thought of all that dancing.
Where would we be without reminiscence
these buzzing sweet cells of golden memory's bloom
mine are nestling within
my photograph album
a treasured time-zone - honeycombed.

Lucy Green

Where Are You?

We used to call him 'Danny Boy'
He filled our life with love and joy
We marvelled at how fast he grew
So quick the days of youth they flew.

Then one day he was not there
We could not find him anywhere
He vanished like the melting snow,
Wherever did our darling go.

I look into the grown up face
But can't see the slightest trace
He looks at me with stranger's eyes
And deep within me something dies.

My heart calls out in mute despair,
My son, dear son, are you in there?
But he kept his distance, far away
From the loving child of yesterday.

It happens oft' that with the years,
A little child just disappears
That lovely lad who once was ours
Has vanished like the summer flowers.

We never saw the shadow creeping
It beckoned him and left us weeping
We turned around and he had gone
Like the dew from the lawn

The world had called and he had grown
For such a little time we own
Those clinging hands and trusting ways
So soon are gone those childhood days.

Thomas Boyle

REJECTED ONE

To the one whom I rejected,
So many years ago,
The love I feel for you now,
You will never know.

Much sorrow we both have known,
Such sadness of the heart,
And my, how the years have flown
Since we were torn apart.

We weren't meant to be together,
That is my belief.
Not meant to comfort one another,
Or share each other's grief.

Tragedy did strike in both our lives,
The experiences differ,
But if I had become your wife,
Things may have turned out better.

Now we are both middle-aged,
Our paths may cross again,
And happiness could be our wage.
I wish I knew just when!

I am Aries, you are Libra,
Both go well together.
'Twas my mistake rejected one,
To have left you for another.

Pat Drew

SENIOR CITIZENS 1996

I have friends who think the same as me,
We ask, why are we here when health fails to be
good and strong, no aches and pains for us,
Instead the niggles, they cause depressions fuss.

Gone are the days when we used to rush about,
Get excited and noisy and sing and shout,
Getting old was years away without a doubt,
All too soon we're aged and grey, and grouch.

We are advised to make the most of the days,
No second chance, rehearsals are for plays,
Trips to clubs and outings, and I must say,
What would we do without them, fade away.

Money really helps if you can't move too well,
Pays for taxi trips if you happen to be frail,
We hate to be a problem to our families it's clear,
Try to be as happy as we can, never fear.

Once a week we have pension day, a big event,
Meet friends for a chat, then sort out the rent,
Put money away for bills, council tax and such,
What's left for food and clothes, not much.

The charity shops do a trade for different clothes,
High fashion not needed for us I suppose,
On the whole our requirements are met,
We can be happy with the bargains we get.

We all know getting old is a worrying time,
The ups and downs costing more than a dime,
But when the weather is bleak and it's a miserable day,
It's bliss to lie in, take breakfast on a tray.

Vi Talman

AFRAID OF THE DARK?

I was afraid of the dark;
I remember times as a child
peering over the edge of blankets
in a bed that in the dark seemed vast
Wondering if tonight at last
the monstrous bogeyman would appear.
I recall how I'd lie
motionless with fear,
believing if I moved I'd die,
and how my heart was thudding so hard
I would clasp my hands over my chest
so that 'it' in the corner wouldn't hear
and tear the offending noise from my breast.

Even now that I'm grown
there are times in the dark
when I think of the bogeyman
and I wonder, what if? As just for a lark
a foot comes from under the duvet,
is slowly lowered to the floor,
and I dare the abomination, that terrible grey
horror lurking under my bed, to claw
at my flesh with its talons.
Just because I've not yet succeeded
in waiting to what happens
doesn't mean my actions are impeded
by a long ago fear of the dark.

Alexander K Stubbs

Joan

I tried to write a poem
about the one I love
The sparkle in her eyes would be
like all the stars above

I would tell about the golden rays
of sunlight in her hair
But I remembered arguments
and heartache and despair

When love we had was tossed aside
and tempers ruled our heads
And cruel words we didn't mean
were better left unsaid

But following the darkest sky
the sun again will shine
And heartache almost seems worthwhile
when our arms once more entwine

Love cannot be taken
from selected lines of prose
It is sometimes like the nettle
not always like the rose

My feelings are not measured
by rhyme or sweet refrain
It is only by the joy I feel
when she is mine again

David Guy Prosser

WITH THIS RING

With this ring, I thee wed'
These words you vowed to me
And promised me a love to last
Throughout life's stormy seas

You were all I ever wanted
And I was proud your wife to be
A gentle heart, a tower of strength
And you loved only me

Our union brought children
Our happiness was complete
My cup was full, I was content
And life was very sweet

But somehow, somewhere I lost you
I did not see the signs
Another stole your love away
And broke this heart of mine

You took my love and crushed it
You broke my faith and trust
My anchor's gone and I'm adrift
And leave you now I must

Till death us do part'
Do you recall
These words you vowed to me?
I remember and with my dying breath
I now set you free

Glenda Greeson

GOODBYE TO A SPECIAL PERSON

(My Mum)

To my darling mum
I feel so sad without you,
My heart feels broken in two.
I thought you would always be here
When you said 'You felt poorly' we said 'You'll be alright'
You were in pain and had such a lot to bear I know that now,
You loved me so much sometimes I did not show it back,
People say the pain gets easier be strong.
Look at your family you have them they depend on you.
I know all these things are true,
But the pain and sadness I feel is really unbearable
It's not easy being able to share things with you.
We go to your grave and put flowers there,
I talk to you and Anita as you are there together
Just to say I love you and be able to put my arms around you
I never thought I would lose you as 63 years old is still young
Spring is here your favourite time of the year.
I want you to rest in heaven,
I hope it's a lovely place where you meet old friends,
Words cannot express how I love you and miss you.
Take care my darling
I will try to be strong
I love you 'Mum'
Goodbye for now.

L E Schoepp

NANA DIED ON THURSDAY

Nana died on Thursday, Michael phoned me up at school,
He'd had an urgent message, he ignored them as a rule,
She'd called us out so often with pains that were not there.
The Doctor said she'd feigned them, though they were the worst she'd swear
Her stomach gave her problems, her headaches were severe,
But her heart it was the strongest so we were not to fear.
And yet they found her sitting, the radio blasting forth,
Her teacup on the carpet, while she sat on the hearth.
They said that she felt nothing, her heart had simply failed,
Yet we both felt guilty, as we stood there shocked and paled.
We'd given her such a talking to about how she should try
To make an effort, join a club, we never thought she'd die!
She was here for lunch on Sunday, on Monday she was pale,
Tuesday we walked her round the green, Wednesday, though feeling frail
Our advice she meekly took and to the Warden's party went,
So our evening visit we forsook and now we sit here grieving
As we never saw her more, her little home we're emptying,
Treasured scatters near and far
Her funeral is on Monday, grandsons bear her to the grave,
Family friends will mourn with us for a generation passed away.

Avrille Oxley McCann

LIFE TOGETHER

I saw him round the neighbourhood,
Never spoke to him, perhaps I should.
Casually we met in the street
And decided that we should have to meet.

Started dating every night,
Walking and talking in the moonlight.
We didn't want ever to part,
It was real true love from the start.

The wedding bells began to chime,
Then I knew that he was mine.
A new life started for both of us
As we finished the day with a fuss.

Three years of happy bliss,
The news of a baby was sealed with a kiss.
A few years later a second baby, what a treat,
It certainly made our family complete.

Thirty seven years of ups and downs,
But our love was stronger we found.
Then one day fate stepped in.
Took you away and left me lonely and grim.

Evelyn M Harding

SILENT TEARS

(For Anne)

No-one sees the silent tears,
That fall like petals soft and clear,
No-one notices the shining eyes glazed with sadness,
At the thought of a departure so near.
No-one sees the thoughts buried deep in my mind,
Of a precious and happy time once spent with you.
These hours and feelings cannot be felt,
But only shared alone, or in written verse to you.
So now walking softly does any emotion lay with sad happiness
At a time so precious, spent once with you.
No-one noticed this emotion pass,
It is only a passing gift for you.
And although we drift with other things to do,
We will always meet again,
And not have to wait in the queue.
There's no attention for me to be needed,
For your strong love is carried with me all the time.
It will pass, as I write more soft falling lines,
Trickling like soft water,
Round, down and over your face.
I hear your footsteps now asking me so clear,
Silent questions,
But no-one ever sees my silent tears,
I felt at times with you.

Louis Crouch

HEART TALK

With you each day that passes by
You show so much love, which you apply
To the special persons in your life,
It would be so great, to call you my wife.

You make so many happy, each and every day
You're the one that makes me feel this way.
I may not be the millionaire you seek,
Perhaps I don't deserve one so very meek.

As each day passes and you're not here,
A need for you, could not be more clear;
When we're together, filled with delight,
Going home alone, dreaming of you all night.

Maybe you think I shouldn't feel this way
How can I tell you what my heart can't say.
If my lips could speak, what's felt inside
My heart I would give, to you, with pride.

If you would care and some time would lend,
I could share with you, my special friend
An inner view of me, that can never be told
Except, the only one, who in my arms enfold.

M G Lowe

INFORMATION

We hope you have enjoyed reading this book - and that you will continue to enjoy it in the coming years.

If you like reading and writing poetry drop us a line, or give us a call, and we'll send you a free information pack.

Write to :-

Arrival Press Information
1-2 Wainman Road
Woodston
Peterborough
PE2 7BU
(01733) 230762

aper